OLYMPIAD WORKBOOK

INTERNATIONAL ENGLISH OLYMPIAD

01 Learning Objectives

02 Multiple Choice Questions

03 HOTS (Achievers Section)

04 Model Test Paper

05 Answer Keys and Solutions

06 OMR Answer Sheet

V&S PUBLISHERS

Published by:

V&S PUBLISHERS

F-2/16, Ansari road, Daryaganj, New Delhi-110002
☎ 23240026, 23240027 • *Fax:* 011-23240028
✉ info@vspublishers.com • ⊕ www.vspublishers.com

 **Online Brandstore: amazon.in/vspublishers**

Regional Office : Hyderabad
5-1-707/1, Brij Bhawan (Beside Central Bank of India Lane)
Bank Street, Koti, Hyderabad - 500 095
☎ 040-24737290
✉ vspublishershyd@gmail.com

Follow us on:   

BUY OUR BOOKS FROM: AMAZON FLIPKART

DISCLAIMER

While every attempt has been made to provide accurate and timely information in this book, neither the author nor the publisher assumes any responsibility for errors, unintended omissions or commissions detected therein. The author and publisher makes no representation or warranty with respect to the comprehensiveness or completeness of the contents provided.

All matters included have been simplified under professional guidance for general information only, without any warranty for applicability on an individual. Any mention of an organization or a website in the book, by way of citation or as a source of additional information, doesn't imply the endorsement of the content either by the author or the publisher. It is possible that websites cited may have changed or removed between the time of editing and publishing the book.

Results from using the expert opinion in this book will be totally dependent on individual circumstances and factors beyond the control of the author and the publisher.

It makes sense to elicit advice from well informed sources before implementing the ideas given in the book. The reader assumes full responsibility for the consequences arising out from reading this book.

For proper guidance, it is advisable to read the book under the watchful eyes of parents/guardian. The buyer of this book assumes all responsibility for the use of given materials and information.

The copyright of the entire content of this book rests with the author/publisher. Any infringement/transmission of the cover design, text or illustrations, in any form, by any means, by any entity will invite legal action and be responsible for consequences thereon.

PUBLISHER'S NOTE

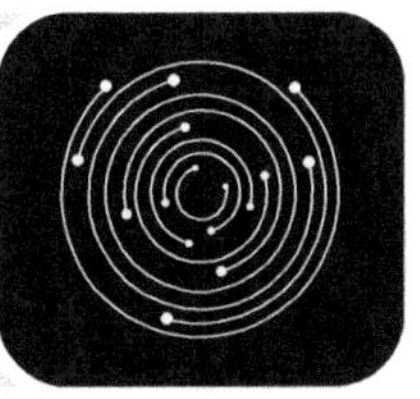

V&S Publishers has carved a significant niche in the publishing industry over the last decade, having successfully published more than 1000 titles across 9 languages spanning over 50 subject categories. Being known for the quality of content, we have built a reputation of excellence and reliability. We have consistently delivered **"Value & Substance"** to our readers, through a wide range of titles across a variety of genres covering school books, fiction and non-fiction that caters to different people from every section of the society.

The **Olympiad Guidebooks for classes 1-10** across all subjects, launched almost a decade ago, under the **GEN X Imprint**, became a go-to-source for the school students in no time, owing to their invaluable and substantive content written in a guidebook pattern,.

Having successfully sold a million copies of the same and in response to demand by both students as well as shopkeepers nationwide; we now present before you our newly launched **Olympiad Workbook Series**, designed for **classes 1-10 across 4 subjects**.

The workbooks are meticulously curated by a team of experienced educators, researchers and subject matter experts, edited by professionals and peer reviewed by teachers. The team has poured its efforts and expertise into creating a crisp and concise workbook which will help and guide the students to the path of success in Olympiad exams. The **MCQs** identified will not only help in scoring top marks in Olympiads but also inculcate a sense of deeper understanding of the subject, by way of solving **HOTS** and referring to complete solutions at the end of the book.

Here we present our new release– **OLYMPIAD WORKBOOK (IEO) CLASS–8** having following features:

- ☞ Based on the latest syllabi
- ☞ MCQs with comprehensive coverage of topics
- ☞ HOTS Questions liberally included
- ☞ A dedicated chapter on logical reasoning
- ☞ Model test paper for thorough practice
- ☞ Sample OMR sheet for real time simulation

We have made sure through our best efforts, that this workbook strictly follows the latest syllabi and patterns of the Olympiad Examination.

As **V&S Publishers** continuously strive to enhance the readability and maintain the credibility of our academic publications, we seek the support of our valuable readers in influencing and enriching the lives of future generations of students.

P.S. While every care has been taken to ensure the correctness of the content, if you come across any error, howsoever minor, do not hesitate to discuss with teachers while pointing that out to us in no uncertain terms.

We wish you all the best for your exams!

DISTINCTIVE FEATURES

01

Learning Objectives

They list the whole chapter as subtopics, helping the teachers to guide children in a step-by-step manner.

02

Multiple Choice Questions

MCQs act as an excellent learning aid, helping you to understand and work on your mistakes.

03

HOTS (Achievers Section)

The High Order Thinking Questions aim to help the student to solve Application-based questions and gain practical understanding of the subject.

04

Model Test Paper

Model test paper are provided at the end of each book, which help the student to test the knowledge which they have gained after thorough reading of all chapters.

05

Answer Key

Detailed Answer Key along with explanations aid the pupil to indentify, understand the mistakes they make during the course of Olympiad preparation.

CONTENTS

SYNONYMS, ANTONYMS, HOMONYMS AND HOMOPHONES

LEARNING OBJECTIVES

➤ Synonyms and Antonyms
➤ Homophones and Homonyms

PRACTICE EXERCISE

I. Choose the option which is synonym of the given words.

1. Abandon
   (A) try   (B) join
   (C) keep with   (D) forsake

2. Abdicate
   (A) join   (B) search
   (C) abandon   (D) advance

3. Absolute
   (A) division   (B) complete
   (C) small   (D) half

4. Abstain
   (A) refrain   (B) ingest
   (C) take in   (D) consume

5. Accord
   (A) confer   (B) refusal
   (C) dissension   (D) opposition

6. Acquaint
   (A) withhold   (B) conceal
   (C) familiarise   (D) risky

7. Aggravate
   (A) decline
   (B) acquire
   (C) excited
   (D) irritate

8. Latent
   (A) apparent   (B) manifest
   (C) concealed   (D) obvious

10. Sporadic
    (A) methodical   (B) continuous
    (C) occasional   (D) constant

II. Choose the option which is opposite of the given words.

11. Indiscreet
    (A) reliable
    (B) honest
    (C) discreet
    (D) stupid

12. Familiar
    (A) unpleasant   (B) dangerous
    (C) friendly   (D) strange

13. Tangible
    (A) intangible   (B) concrete
    (C) actual   (D) solid

14. Love
    (A) villainy
    (B) hatred
    (C) compulsion
    (D) force

15. Famous
    (A) disgraced
    (B) unknown
    (C) evil
    (D) popular
16. Absolute
    (A) deficient
    (B) faulty
    (C) limited
    (D) scarce
17. Frugal
    (A) copious
    (B) extravagant
    (C) generous
    (D) ostentatious
18. Insipid
    (A) tasty
    (B) stupid
    (C) discreet
    (D) feast
19. Able
    (A) disable
    (B) inable
    (C) unable
    (D) misable
20. Hostility
    (A) courtesy
    (B) hospitality
    (C) relationship
    (D) friendliness

III. Fill in the blanks with the correct option.

21. I didn't ____ what she said.
    (A) hear
    (B) here
    (C) knew
    (D) known
22. They forgot to take ____ printouts.
    (A) there
    (B) their
    (C) they're
    (D) none of these

23. Venison is the meat from a ____.
    (A) dear
    (B) deer
    (C) cow
    (D) camel
24. The house is by the ____.
    (A) see
    (B) sea
    (C) saw
    (B) seen
25. She held the ____ in her hand.
    (A) reigns
    (B) rains
    (C) reins
    (D) none of these
26. They tried to ____ the painting.
    (A) steel
    (B) steal
    (C) stole
    (B) stolen
27. He had to ____ the button on.
    (A) sow
    (B) sew
    (C) either (A) or (B)
    (D) none of these
28. I hope the ____ is fine.
    (A) weather
    (B) whether
    (C) wether
    (D) none of these
29. He was a medieval ____.
    (A) night
    (B) knight
    (C) man
    (D) person
30. The building ____ is huge.
    (A) site
    (B) sight
    (C) scene
    (D) view

Choose the correct synonym from the options below.

31. Beautiful
    (A) Bright   (B) Pretty
    (C) Mirthful   (D) Gracious

32. Hardworking
    (A) Content   (B) Fair
    (C) Sincere   (D) Diligent

33. Lazy
    (A) Secure   (B) Lethargic
    (C) Opportunist   (D) Withdrawn

34. Outgoing
    (A) Extrovert
    (B) Attractive
    (C) Objective
    (D) Trustworthy

35. Amiable
    (A) Determined
    (B) Sharp
    (C) Kind
    (D) Lovely

—Darken Your Choice with HB Pencil—

1.	Ⓐ Ⓑ Ⓒ Ⓓ	8.	Ⓐ Ⓑ Ⓒ Ⓓ	15.	Ⓐ Ⓑ Ⓒ Ⓓ	22	Ⓐ Ⓑ Ⓒ Ⓓ	29.	Ⓐ Ⓑ Ⓒ Ⓓ
2.	Ⓐ Ⓑ Ⓒ Ⓓ	9.	Ⓐ Ⓑ Ⓒ Ⓓ	16.	Ⓐ Ⓑ Ⓒ Ⓓ	23.	Ⓐ Ⓑ Ⓒ Ⓓ	30.	Ⓐ Ⓑ Ⓒ Ⓓ
3.	Ⓐ Ⓑ Ⓒ Ⓓ	10.	Ⓐ Ⓑ Ⓒ Ⓓ	17.	Ⓐ Ⓑ Ⓒ Ⓓ	24.	Ⓐ Ⓑ Ⓒ Ⓓ	31.	Ⓐ Ⓑ Ⓒ Ⓓ
4.	Ⓐ Ⓑ Ⓒ Ⓓ	11.	Ⓐ Ⓑ Ⓒ Ⓓ	18.	Ⓐ Ⓑ Ⓒ Ⓓ	25.	Ⓐ Ⓑ Ⓒ Ⓓ	32.	Ⓐ Ⓑ Ⓒ Ⓓ
5.	Ⓐ Ⓑ Ⓒ Ⓓ	12.	Ⓐ Ⓑ Ⓒ Ⓓ	19.	Ⓐ Ⓑ Ⓒ Ⓓ	26.	Ⓐ Ⓑ Ⓒ Ⓓ	33.	Ⓐ Ⓑ Ⓒ Ⓓ
6.	Ⓐ Ⓑ Ⓒ Ⓓ	13.	Ⓐ Ⓑ Ⓒ Ⓓ	20.	Ⓐ Ⓑ Ⓒ Ⓓ	27.	Ⓐ Ⓑ Ⓒ Ⓓ	34.	Ⓐ Ⓑ Ⓒ Ⓓ
7.	Ⓐ Ⓑ Ⓒ Ⓓ	14.	Ⓐ Ⓑ Ⓒ Ⓓ	21.	Ⓐ Ⓑ Ⓒ Ⓓ	28.	Ⓐ Ⓑ Ⓒ Ⓓ	35.	Ⓐ Ⓑ Ⓒ Ⓓ

ANALOGIES AND SPELLINGS

➤ Analogy and its types
➤ Rules of Spelling

PRACTICE EXERCISE

I. Choose the option that best matches the analogy.

1. Drip : Gush
   (A) Cry : Laugh
   (B) Curl : Roll
   (C) Stream : Tributary
   (D) Dent : Destroy

2. Walk : Legs
   (A) Gleam : Eyes
   (B) Chew : Mouth
   (C) Dress : Hem
   (D) Cover : Book

3. Enfranchise : Slavery
   (A) Equation : Mathematics
   (B) Liberate : Confine
   (C) Bondage : Subjugation
   (D) Appeasement : Unreasonable

4. Union jack : Vexillology
   (A) Toad : Ornithology
   (B) Turtle : Microbiology
   (C) Gymnosperms : Botany
   (D) Friend : home Economics

5. Topaz : Yellow
   (A) Diamond : Carat
   (B) Jeweler : Clarity
   (C) Sapphire : Red
   (D) Amethyst : Purple

6.
   (A) Adulation   (B) Adlation
   (C) Aduletion   (D) Addulation

7.
   (A) Adulterate   (B) Adeldurate
   (C) Adulterat   (D) Adultarate

8.
   (A) Adventitious   (B) Adventitous
   (C) Adventitus   (D) Adventituous

9.
   (A) Advercity   (B) Advercety
   (C) Adversity   (D) Advercity

10.
   (A) Affedevit   (B) Afidevit
   (C) Affidevit   (D) Affidavit

II. Find out the alternative which will replace the question mark.

11. Cup : Lip :: Bird : ?
    (A) Bush   (B) Grass
    (C) Forest   (D) Beak

12. Flow : River :: Stagnant : ?
    (A) Rain   (B) Stream
    (C) Pool   (D) Canal

13. Paw : Cat :: Hoof : ?
    (A) Lamb   (B) Elephant
    (C) Lion   (D) Horse

14. Ornithologist : Bird :: Archaeologist : ?
   (A) Islands
   (B) Mediators
   (C) Archealogy
   (D) Aquatic

15. Peacock : India :: Bear : ?
   (A) Australia   (B) America
   (C) Russia   (D) England

16. I hope to ______ my own business one day.
   (A) do   (B) have
   (C) make   (D) has

17. I don't ______ many hobbies.
   (A) do   (B) have
   (C) make   (D) has

18. My wife usually ______ the bed, rather than me.
   (A) does   (B) has
   (C) makes   (D) have

19. Many countries ______ problems with obesity.
   (A) do   (B) have
   (C) make   (D) has

20. I ______ a mistake in my IELTS reading the last time I took the test.
   (A) did   (B) had
   (C) made   (D) has

III. Choose the correct one word substitution for the given word/sentence.

21. Extreme old age when a man behaves like a fool
   (A) Imbecility
   (B) Senility
   (C) Dotage
   (D) Superannuation

22. That which cannot be corrected
   (A) Unintelligible   (B) Indelible
   (C) Illegible   (D) Incorrigible

23. The study of ancient societies
   (A) Anthropology   (B) Archaeology
   (C) History   (D) Ethnology

24. A person of good understanding knowledge and reasoning power
   (A) Expert   (B) Intellectual
   (C) Snob   (D) Literate

25. A person who insists on something
   (A) Disciplinarian   (B) Stickler
   (C) Instantaneous   (D) Boaster

26. I'm an ______ admirer of your work.
   (A) ardent   (B) triumphant
   (C) stale   (D) considerable

27. This new process is a ______ advance in technology.
   (A) ardent
   (B) significant
   (C) stale
   (D) considerable

28. He knows the interviewer already and that will give him an ______ advantage over me.
   (A) ardent   (B) significant
   (C) unfair   (D) considerable

29. I wouldn't upset him. He can be a ______ adversary.
   (A) ardent   (B) significant
   (C) unfair   (D) dangerous

30. He gave me some ______ advice and I took it.
   (A) ardent   (B) significant
   (C) unfair   (D) blunt

In sentence below, one word has been printed in bold type which is wrongly spelt. Choose the correctly spelt word.

31. His life is so hectic that he is prepared to be tolerant of trivial **pecadillos**.
    (A) pecedillos   (B) pecedilos
    (C) peccadillos   (D) peccadillos

32. The weather is so hot that I am feeling full of **longour**.
    (A) languor   (B) langur
    (C) langoor   (D) languor

33. It was an unexpected **denuement** in the play performed by the artists.
    (A) denoument   (B) denuemant
    (C) denuement   (D) denouement

34. A person living permanently in a certain place
    (A) Resident   (B) Native
    (C) Domicile   (D) Subject

35. Mania for stealing articles
    (A) Hypomania   (B) Kleptomania
    (C) Logomania   (D) Stelomania

Darken Your Choice with HB Pencil

1. Ⓐ Ⓑ Ⓒ Ⓓ	8. Ⓐ Ⓑ Ⓒ Ⓓ	15. Ⓐ Ⓑ Ⓒ Ⓓ	22 Ⓐ Ⓑ Ⓒ Ⓓ	29. Ⓐ Ⓑ Ⓒ Ⓓ
2. Ⓐ Ⓑ Ⓒ Ⓓ	9. Ⓐ Ⓑ Ⓒ Ⓓ	16. Ⓐ Ⓑ Ⓒ Ⓓ	23. Ⓐ Ⓑ Ⓒ Ⓓ	30. Ⓐ Ⓑ Ⓒ Ⓓ
3. Ⓐ Ⓑ Ⓒ Ⓓ	10. Ⓐ Ⓑ Ⓒ Ⓓ	17. Ⓐ Ⓑ Ⓒ Ⓓ	24. Ⓐ Ⓑ Ⓒ Ⓓ	31. Ⓐ Ⓑ Ⓒ Ⓓ
4. Ⓐ Ⓑ Ⓒ Ⓓ	11. Ⓐ Ⓑ Ⓒ Ⓓ	18. Ⓐ Ⓑ Ⓒ Ⓓ	25. Ⓐ Ⓑ Ⓒ Ⓓ	32. Ⓐ Ⓑ Ⓒ Ⓓ
5. Ⓐ Ⓑ Ⓒ Ⓓ	12. Ⓐ Ⓑ Ⓒ Ⓓ	19. Ⓐ Ⓑ Ⓒ Ⓓ	26. Ⓐ Ⓑ Ⓒ Ⓓ	33. Ⓐ Ⓑ Ⓒ Ⓓ
6. Ⓐ Ⓑ Ⓒ Ⓓ	13. Ⓐ Ⓑ Ⓒ Ⓓ	20. Ⓐ Ⓑ Ⓒ Ⓓ	27. Ⓐ Ⓑ Ⓒ Ⓓ	34. Ⓐ Ⓑ Ⓒ Ⓓ
7. Ⓐ Ⓑ Ⓒ Ⓓ	14. Ⓐ Ⓑ Ⓒ Ⓓ	21. Ⓐ Ⓑ Ⓒ Ⓓ	28. Ⓐ Ⓑ Ⓒ Ⓓ	35. Ⓐ Ⓑ Ⓒ Ⓓ

ONE WORD

LEARNING OBJECTIVES

➤ Concept and usage of One Words

PRACTICE EXERCISE

I. Choose the option that best matches the analogy.

1. Lumen : Brightness
   (A) Candle : Light
   (B) Density : Darkness
   (C) Nickel : Metal
   (D) Inches : Length

2. Maceration : Liquid
   (A) Sublimation : Gas
   (B) Evaporation : Humidity
   (C) Trail : Path
   (D) Erosion : Weather

3. Clumsy : Botch
   (A) Wicked : Insinuate
   (B) Strict : Pamper
   (C) Willful : Heed
   (D) Lazy : Shirk

4. Fugitive : Flee
   (A) Parasite : Foster
   (B) Braggart : Boast
   (C) Sage : Stifle
   (D) Bystander : Procure

5. Chronological : Time
   (A) Virtual : Truth
   (B) Abnormal : Value
   (C) Marginal : Knowledge
   (D) Ordinal : Place

6. Soot : Grimy
   (A) Frost : Transparent
   (B) Sunshine : Fruitless
   (C) Rain : Sodden
   (D) Pall : Gaudy

7. Morbid : Unfavorable
   (A) Reputable : Favorable
   (B) Maternal : Unfavorable
   (C) Disputatious : Favorable
   (D) Vigilant : Unfavorable

8. Sullen : Brood
   (A) Lethargic : Cavort
   (B) Regal : Cringe
   (C) Docile : Obey
   (D) Poised : Blunder

9. Author : Literate
   (A) Cynic : Gullible
   (B) Hothead : Prudent
   (C) Saint : Notorious
   (D) Judge : Impartial

10. Massive : Bulk
    (A) Ultimate : Magnitude
    (B) Trivial : Importance
    (C) Anonymous : Luster
    (D) Gigantic : Size

II. **Find out the alternative which will replace the question mark.**

11. Reason : Sebtpo :: Think : ?
    (A) Sghmj (B) Uijol
    (C) Uhnki (D) Ujkpm

12. Carbon : Diamond :: Corundum : ?
    (A) Garnet (B) Ruby
    (C) Pukhraj (D) Pearl

13. Nation : Antino :: Hungry : ?
    (A) Hnugry (B) Uhngyr
    (C) Yrnguh (D) Unhgyr

14. Architect : Building :: Sculptor : ?
    (A) Museum (B) Stone
    (C) Chisel (D) Statue

15. Eye : Myopia :: Teeth : ?
    (A) Pyorrhoea (B) Cataract
    (C) Trachoma (D) Eczema

16. Conference : Chairman :: Newspaper : ?
    (A) Reporter (B) Distributor
    (C) Printer (D) Editor

17. Safe : Secure :: Protect : ?
    (A) Lock (B) Sure
    (C) Guard (D) Conserve

18. Master : Ocuvgt :: Labour : ?
    (A) Ncdqwt (B) Nderwt
    (C) Nberwt (D) Nedrwt

19. Microphone : Loud :: Microscope : ?
    (A) Elongate (B) Investigate
    (C) Magnify (D) Examine

20. Melt : Liquid :: Freeze : ?
    (A) Ice (B) Condense
    (C) Solid (D) Force

III. **Choose the correct one word substitution for the given word/sentence.**

21. State in which the few govern the many
    (A) Monarchy (B) Oligarchy
    (C) Plutocracy (D) Autocracy

22. A style in which a writer makes a display of his knowledge
    (A) Pedantic (B) Verbose
    (C) Pompous (D) Ornate

23. Words inscribed on tomb
    (A) Epitome (B) Epistle
    (C) Epilogue (D) Epitaph

24. One who eats everything
    (A) Omnivorous (B) Omniscient
    (C) Irrestible (D) Insolvent

25. The custom or practice of having more than one husband at same time
    (A) Polygyny (B) Polyphony
    (C) Polyandry (D) Polychromy

26. Tending to move away from the centre or axis
    (A) Centrifugal
    (B) Centripetal
    (C) Axiomatic
    (D) Awry

27. A person interested in collecting, studying and selling of old things
    (A) Antiquarian
    (B) Junk-dealer
    (C) Crank
    (D) Archealogist

28. That which cannot be seen
    (A) Insensible (B) Intangible
    (C) Invisible (D) Unseen

29. To slap with a flat object
    (A) Chop (B) Hew
    (C) Gnaw (D) Swat

30. Habitually silent or talking little
    (A) Servile
    (B) Unequivocal
    (C) Taciturn
    (D) Synoptic

Choose the correct one word for given sentences.

31. One who loves mankind is called
    (A) Optimist   (B) Philanthropist
    (C) Optometrist   (D) Truant

32. A Government run by a dictator is termed as
    (A) Autocracy   (B) Democracy
    (C) Oligracy   (D) Theocracy

33. A remedy for all disease is
    (A) Medicine
    (B) Medical
    (C) Medica
    (D) Panacea

—Darken Your Choice with HB Pencil—

1.	Ⓐ Ⓑ Ⓒ Ⓓ	8.	Ⓐ Ⓑ Ⓒ Ⓓ	15.	Ⓐ Ⓑ Ⓒ Ⓓ	22	Ⓐ Ⓑ Ⓒ Ⓓ	29.	Ⓐ Ⓑ Ⓒ Ⓓ
2.	Ⓐ Ⓑ Ⓒ Ⓓ	9.	Ⓐ Ⓑ Ⓒ Ⓓ	16.	Ⓐ Ⓑ Ⓒ Ⓓ	23.	Ⓐ Ⓑ Ⓒ Ⓓ	30.	Ⓐ Ⓑ Ⓒ Ⓓ
3.	Ⓐ Ⓑ Ⓒ Ⓓ	10.	Ⓐ Ⓑ Ⓒ Ⓓ	17.	Ⓐ Ⓑ Ⓒ Ⓓ	24.	Ⓐ Ⓑ Ⓒ Ⓓ	31.	Ⓐ Ⓑ Ⓒ Ⓓ
4.	Ⓐ Ⓑ Ⓒ Ⓓ	11.	Ⓐ Ⓑ Ⓒ Ⓓ	18.	Ⓐ Ⓑ Ⓒ Ⓓ	25.	Ⓐ Ⓑ Ⓒ Ⓓ	32.	Ⓐ Ⓑ Ⓒ Ⓓ
5.	Ⓐ Ⓑ Ⓒ Ⓓ	12.	Ⓐ Ⓑ Ⓒ Ⓓ	19.	Ⓐ Ⓑ Ⓒ Ⓓ	26.	Ⓐ Ⓑ Ⓒ Ⓓ	33.	Ⓐ Ⓑ Ⓒ Ⓓ
6.	Ⓐ Ⓑ Ⓒ Ⓓ	13.	Ⓐ Ⓑ Ⓒ Ⓓ	20.	Ⓐ Ⓑ Ⓒ Ⓓ	27.	Ⓐ Ⓑ Ⓒ Ⓓ		
7.	Ⓐ Ⓑ Ⓒ Ⓓ	14.	Ⓐ Ⓑ Ⓒ Ⓓ	21.	Ⓐ Ⓑ Ⓒ Ⓓ	28.	Ⓐ Ⓑ Ⓒ Ⓓ		

PHRASAL VERBS, IDIOMS AND PROVERBS

LEARNING OBJECTIVES

➤ Concept of Phrasal Verbs
➤ Types of Phrasal Verbs

PRACTICE EXERCISE

I. Fill in the blanks with correct option.

1. Robert was expected to arrive at 8 o'clock, but he didn't turn _______ until midnight.
   (A) out (B) up
   (C) off (D) with

2. Peter needs either to get a raise or to get a better job, because he can't get _______ on his current salary.
   (A) by (B) out
   (C) in (D) off

3. Manuela and Glenda didn't like each other at first, but now they get _______.
   (A) over
   (B) across
   (C) away
   (D) along

4. The plane is scheduled to take _______ at 7 a.m.
   (A) away (B) to
   (C) off (D) with

5. We need milk, but we can do _______ beer.
   (A) without (B) along
   (C) away (D) off

6. The wedding was originally scheduled for June 12, but it has been put _______ until September 24.
   (A) out (B) away
   (C) off (D) up

7. Our alarm clock is set to go _______ at 6 a.m.
   (A) away (B) up
   (C) out (D) off

8. Gary asked Cynthia to marry him, but she turned him _______.
   (A) down (B) without
   (C) across (D) over

9. The emergency workers managed to put _______ the fire.
   (A) off (B) out
   (C) down (D) without

10. Everyone thought she was English, but she turned _______ to be Canadian.
    (A) up (B) off
    (C) by (D) out

II. Choose the correct option for the given proverb/idiom.

11. To make clean breast of
    (A) To gain prominence
    (B) To praise oneself
    (C) To confess without reserve
    (D) To destroy before it blooms

12. To keeps one's temper
    (A) To become hungry
    (B) To be in good mood
    (C) To preserve ones energy
    (D) To be aloof from

13. To catch a tartar
(A) To trap wanted criminal with great difficulty
(B) To catch a dangerous person
(C) To meet with disaster
(D) To deal with a person who is more than one's match

14. To drive home
(A) To find one's roots
(B) To return to place of rest
(C) Back to original position
(D) To emphasise

15. To have an axe to grind
(A) A private end to serve
(B) To fail to arouse interest
(C) To have no result
(D) To work for both sides

16. To cry wolf
(A) To listen eagerly
(B) To give false alarm
(C) To turn pale
(D) To keep off starvation

17. To end in smoke
(A) To make completely understand
(B) To ruin oneself
(C) To excite great applause
(D) To overcome someone

18. To be above board
(A) To have a good height
(B) To be honest in any business deal
(C) They have no debts
(D) To try to be beautiful

19. To put one's hand to plough
(A) To take up agricultural farming
(B) To take a difficult task
(C) To get entangled into unnecessary things
(D) Take interest in technical work

20. To pick holes
(A) To find some reason to quarrel
(B) To destroy something
(C) To criticise someone
(D) To cut some part of an item

III. Choose the most appropriate option which explains the given idiom/phrase.

21. Bid defiance
(A) to obey
(B) to ignore
(C) to follow
(D) none of these

22. Blow one's trumpet
(A) To praise other
(B) To praise leader
(C) To praise ownself
(D) To praise community

23. Bury the hatchet
(A) to break peace
(B) joint operation of killing
(C) to make peace
(D) none of these

24. Bring to book
(A) To punish
(B) To serve
(C) To praise
(D) To write a story

25. Blaze the trail
(A) To stop a movement
(B) To join a movement
(C) To protect a movement
(D) To start a movement

26. Broken Reed
(A) Continue support
(B) Support that failed
(C) Support endlessly
(D) None of these

27. By dint of
(A) By force of
(B) By permission of
(C) By fear of
(D) By blessing of

28. Charley horse
(A) Very rapid
(B) Very weak
(C) Stiffness
(D) Boldness

29. Cart before the horse
    (A) To be ready to go
    (B) To be very active
    (C) To do things in reverse order
    (D) To do things in right order

30. Chalk and Cheese
    (A) Different from each other
    (B) Having same properties
    (C) Having fun together
    (D) Making plans

HOTS (ACHIEVERS SECTION)

Read the passages and choose the correct phrasal verbs that can replace the underlined portions/blanks.

31. Once the verdict of guilty was ___1___, Tarun ___2___ to prove that his brother ___3___ for a crime that he did not commit.
    (A) Handed in   (B) Handed out
    (C) Handed down   (D) Handed

32. Once the verdict of guilty was ___1___, Tarun ___2___ to prove that his brother ___3___ for a crime that he did not commit.
    (A) Waited about   (B) Planned about
    (C) Set about   (D) Wished about

33. Once the verdict of guilty was ___1___, Tarun ___2___ to prove that his brother ___3___ for a crime that he did not commit.
    (A) Frames
    (B) Are framed
    (C) Framed
    (D) Had been framed

34. You will never ___4___ anything if you continue ___5___ with that bunch of dropouts," said the Principal to Karun.
    (A) Meet up with   (B) Achieve to
    (C) Amount to   (D) Refer to

35. You will never ______4______ anything if you continue ______5______with that bunch of dropouts," said the Principal to Karun.
    (A) Hanging about   (B) Hanging out
    (C) Hanging by   (D) Hanging for

	A B C D		A B C D		A B C D		A B C D		A B C D
1.	Ⓐ Ⓑ Ⓒ Ⓓ	8.	Ⓐ Ⓑ Ⓒ Ⓓ	15.	Ⓐ Ⓑ Ⓒ Ⓓ	22	Ⓐ Ⓑ Ⓒ Ⓓ	29.	Ⓐ Ⓑ Ⓒ Ⓓ
2.	Ⓐ Ⓑ Ⓒ Ⓓ	9.	Ⓐ Ⓑ Ⓒ Ⓓ	16.	Ⓐ Ⓑ Ⓒ Ⓓ	23.	Ⓐ Ⓑ Ⓒ Ⓓ	30.	Ⓐ Ⓑ Ⓒ Ⓓ
3.	Ⓐ Ⓑ Ⓒ Ⓓ	10.	Ⓐ Ⓑ Ⓒ Ⓓ	17.	Ⓐ Ⓑ Ⓒ Ⓓ	24.	Ⓐ Ⓑ Ⓒ Ⓓ	31.	Ⓐ Ⓑ Ⓒ Ⓓ
4.	Ⓐ Ⓑ Ⓒ Ⓓ	11.	Ⓐ Ⓑ Ⓒ Ⓓ	18.	Ⓐ Ⓑ Ⓒ Ⓓ	25.	Ⓐ Ⓑ Ⓒ Ⓓ	32.	Ⓐ Ⓑ Ⓒ Ⓓ
5.	Ⓐ Ⓑ Ⓒ Ⓓ	12.	Ⓐ Ⓑ Ⓒ Ⓓ	19.	Ⓐ Ⓑ Ⓒ Ⓓ	26.	Ⓐ Ⓑ Ⓒ Ⓓ	33.	Ⓐ Ⓑ Ⓒ Ⓓ
6.	Ⓐ Ⓑ Ⓒ Ⓓ	13.	Ⓐ Ⓑ Ⓒ Ⓓ	20.	Ⓐ Ⓑ Ⓒ Ⓓ	27.	Ⓐ Ⓑ Ⓒ Ⓓ	34.	Ⓐ Ⓑ Ⓒ Ⓓ
7.	Ⓐ Ⓑ Ⓒ Ⓓ	14.	Ⓐ Ⓑ Ⓒ Ⓓ	21.	Ⓐ Ⓑ Ⓒ Ⓓ	28.	Ⓐ Ⓑ Ⓒ Ⓓ	35.	Ⓐ Ⓑ Ⓒ Ⓓ

NOUNS AND PRONOUNS

LEARNING OBJECTIVES

➤ Kinds of Nouns
➤ Usage of Nouns
➤ Usage of Pronoun

PRACTICE EXERCISE

I. Fill in the blanks with the correct option.

1. There was a robbery at the ABC Bank. The thief ran off with a large _________ of cash.
   (A) pod   (B) deck
   (C) bundle   (D) none of these

2. For Christmas, I received in the mail a small _________ from my cousin. She sent me a woolen scarf.
   (A) deck   (B) parcel
   (C) crowd   (D) none of these

3. There was a _______ of cars on the road.
   (A) fleet   (B) nest
   (C) swarm   (D) none of these

4. The man never cleaned his office. He left a _________ of files and papers on his desk.
   (A) army   (B) archipelago
   (C) stack   (D) none of these

5. My friend's cat had a __________ of kittens on the weekend.
   (A) gaggle   (B) litter
   (C) swarm   (D) none of these

6. On Sunday, I went to Stanley Park and saw a _______ of dolphins in Lost Lagoon.
   (A) drove   (B) school
   (C) brood   (D) none of these

7. At the library, there is a _________ of useful educational resources, such as: books, audio tapes, dictionaries, computers, etc.
   (A) host   (B) litter
   (C) nest   (D) none of these

8. I was attacked by a _______ of bees.
   (A) swarm   (B) deck
   (C) package   (D) none of these

9. On the ferry ride from Victoria, I saw a _________ of whales in the ocean.
   (A) bundle   (B) pack
   (C) pod   (D) none of these

10. On a clear summer night you can see a _________ of stars.
    (A) galaxy   (B) school
    (C) pod   (D) none of these

II. Fill in the blanks with correct pronoun in the following sentences.

11. Gary's mom asked _______ to clean the garage.
    (A) he   (B) him
    (C) her   (D) his

12. A student at an all boys high school should be on ______ best behavior.
    (A) their   (B) his
    (C) him   (D) her

13. Neither Mary nor ______ knew why the store was closed.
   (A) I   (B) me
   (C) his   (D) her
14. After school you and ____ must discuss a few things.
   (A) I   (B) me
   (C) him   (D) her
15. Everyone at the table has eaten ________ lunch earlier.
   (A) his or her   (B) their
   (C) me   (D) its

III. Find out the pronoun(s) in each sentence and choose the correct option.

16. When I looked over at the man, I noticed that he was reading a book.
   (A) I
   (B) I, he
   (C) him
   (D) none of these
17. I did not know the right answer.
   (A) him
   (B) I
   (C) answer
   (D) none of these
18. Why don't you go outside?
   (A) you   (B) outside
   (c) go   (D) none of these
16. Take Raman with you.
   (A) me   (B) take
   (C) you   (D) none of these
20. I like running fast.
   (A) I   (B) run
   (C) run   (D) none of these

IV. Fill in the blank with the right pronoun.

21. Did he see ___?
   (A) us   (B) we
   (C) she   (D) i
22. I took the bag from ____.
   (A) him   (B) they
   (C) his   (D) hers
23. My brother and ___ went to the park?
   (A) I   (B) us
   (C) our   (D) me
24. What did ____ do about the car?
   (A) them   (B) they
   (C) us   (D) he
25. What did ____ say about the work?
   (A) she   (B) me
   (C) their   (D) him
26. Where will ___ go from here?
   (A) you   (B) us
   (C) our   (D) their
27. Can ____ talk for a minute?
   (A) we   (B) us
   (C) him   (D) me
28. Is this house ____?
   (A) theirs   (B) them
   (C) him   (D) me
29. Why don't ____ have a seat?
   (A) you   (B) us
   (C) her   (D) them
30. Is that cup ____?
   (A) his   (B) him
   (C) my   (D) our

I. Fill in the blanks with the correct noun.

31. On my African trip, I saw a _________ of lions.
    (A) bundle
    (B) pride
    (C) pack
    (D) none of these

32. I had so much fun in Hawaii swimming with a _________ of fish.
    (A) army
    (B) school
    (C) bevy
    (D) none of these

33. I like to play card games. So when I go camping, I usually take a _______ of cards with me.
    (A) school
    (B) pack
    (C) herd
    (D) none of these

34. I have lost a _______ of keys.
    (A) hive
    (B) chain
    (C) bunch
    (D) none of these

35. There seems to be a plan behind this chain of _______.
    (A) goodness
    (B) series
    (C) events
    (D) none of these

Darken Your Choice with HB Pencil

1.	Ⓐ Ⓑ Ⓒ Ⓓ	8.	Ⓐ Ⓑ Ⓒ Ⓓ	15.	Ⓐ Ⓑ Ⓒ Ⓓ	22	Ⓐ Ⓑ Ⓒ Ⓓ	29.	Ⓐ Ⓑ Ⓒ Ⓓ
2.	Ⓐ Ⓑ Ⓒ Ⓓ	9.	Ⓐ Ⓑ Ⓒ Ⓓ	16.	Ⓐ Ⓑ Ⓒ Ⓓ	23.	Ⓐ Ⓑ Ⓒ Ⓓ	30.	Ⓐ Ⓑ Ⓒ Ⓓ
3.	Ⓐ Ⓑ Ⓒ Ⓓ	10.	Ⓐ Ⓑ Ⓒ Ⓓ	17.	Ⓐ Ⓑ Ⓒ Ⓓ	24.	Ⓐ Ⓑ Ⓒ Ⓓ	31.	Ⓐ Ⓑ Ⓒ Ⓓ
4.	Ⓐ Ⓑ Ⓒ Ⓓ	11.	Ⓐ Ⓑ Ⓒ Ⓓ	18.	Ⓐ Ⓑ Ⓒ Ⓓ	25.	Ⓐ Ⓑ Ⓒ Ⓓ	32.	Ⓐ Ⓑ Ⓒ Ⓓ
5.	Ⓐ Ⓑ Ⓒ Ⓓ	12.	Ⓐ Ⓑ Ⓒ Ⓓ	19.	Ⓐ Ⓑ Ⓒ Ⓓ	26.	Ⓐ Ⓑ Ⓒ Ⓓ	33.	Ⓐ Ⓑ Ⓒ Ⓓ
6.	Ⓐ Ⓑ Ⓒ Ⓓ	13.	Ⓐ Ⓑ Ⓒ Ⓓ	20.	Ⓐ Ⓑ Ⓒ Ⓓ	27.	Ⓐ Ⓑ Ⓒ Ⓓ	34.	Ⓐ Ⓑ Ⓒ Ⓓ
7.	Ⓐ Ⓑ Ⓒ Ⓓ	14.	Ⓐ Ⓑ Ⓒ Ⓓ	21.	Ⓐ Ⓑ Ⓒ Ⓓ	28.	Ⓐ Ⓑ Ⓒ Ⓓ	35.	Ⓐ Ⓑ Ⓒ Ⓓ

VERBS AND ADVERBS

LEARNING OBJECTIVES

➤ Verbs and its different types

➤ Modal Auxiliaries

PRACTICE EXERCISE

I. Fill in the blanks with the correct option.

1. Have you ever ___ abroad?
   (A) go (B) went
   (B) to (D) been

2. She's ___ a shower at the moment.
   (A) taking (B) taken
   (C) take (D) takes

3. I always ___ before bed.
   (A) reading (B) read
   (C) to read (D) none of these

4. He will ___ you later.
   (A) to call (B) calls
   (C) calling (D) call

5. I don't know who ___ the chair.
   (A) break (B) broke
   (C) breaking (D) breaks

6. We've all been ___ about you.
   (A) to think (B) thought
   (C) thinking (D) thinks

7. Someone ___ moved my bag.
   (A) have (B) having
   (C) has (D) haves

8. We ___ playing cards all afternoon.
   (A) were (B) was
   (C) be (D) is

9. Those ___ the type I like.
   (A) isn't (B) don't
   (C) won't (D) aren't

10. James asked me ___ him.
    (A) to email (B) emailing
    (C) emailed (D) email

II. Fill in the blanks with the correct option.

11. He seems really competent but he's not. But he appears so assured that he'll _______ in a lot of people.
    (A) set (B) take
    (C) put (D) get

12. It's a really big assignment. I'm going to have to _______ in a lot of hard work.
    (A) set (B) call
    (C) put (D) get

13. You'll need to be able to demonstrate this without any errors so if I were you I'd _______ in some practice beforehand.
    (A) set (B) call
    (C) come (D) get

14. That's the usual company policy but it's not something that is _______ in stone.
    (A) set (B) call
    (C) put (D) get

15. There are 120 applicants for every vacancy so it's not very easy to _______ in.
    (A) call (B) get
    (C) put (D) give

III. Fill in the blanks with the correct option.

16. _________ I met my childhood friend Meeta.
    (A) Yesterday   (B) Tomorrow
    (C) This Sunday   (D) none of these

17. You need to run _______to win this race.
    (A) slow   (B) steadily
    (C) fast   (D) none of these

18. I won't say it _________.
    (A) progressively   (B) repeatedly
    (C) necessarily   (D) none of these

19. Speak _________, I cannot hear you.
    (A) loudly   (B) slowly
    (C) hardly   (D) none of these

20. You should _______ smoke as it is dangerous for your health.
    (A) always   (B) usually
    (C) never   (D) none of these

IV. Fill in the blanks with the most appropriate option.

21. When my teacher talks too ___, it's difficult to understand him.
    (A) quickly
    (B) quietly
    (C) slowly
    (D) none of these

22. I always study ___ for a big test.
    (A) goodly   (B) hardly
    (C) hard   (D) none of these

23. My dad used to shout ___ when he was angry.
    (A) loudly   (B) noise
    (C) loud   (D) none of these

24. Please try to behave ___ when you meet my family.
    (A) quickly   (B) softly
    (C) normally   (D) none of these

25. She did ___ in her tennis match last week. She won.
    (A) bad   (B) goodly
    (C) well   (D) none of these

V. Fill in the blanks by selecting the best adverb of frequency from the given options.

26. Carlos is an excellent student. He _______ goes to class.
    (A) always   (B) usually
    (C) sometimes   (D) seldom
    (E) never

27. I hate vegetables. I _________ eat carrots.
    (A) always   (B) usually
    (C) sometimes   (D) never

28. Robert goes to the gym only two or three times a year. He _______ goes to the gym.
    (A) always   (B) never
    (C) usually   (D) seldom

29. Harold never leaves the college on Friday. He _______ eats at the cafeteria on Fridays.
    (A) always   (B) never
    (C) seldom   (D) none

30. Ms. Biethan is always in a good mood. She is _________ sad.
    (A) always   (B) usually
    (C) never   (D) none of these

I. Fill in the blanks with the correct verb.

31. I knew he would get promoted. It's good to see him _______ up the ladder.
    (A) speak
    (B) move
    (C) gee
    (D) throw

32. They badly need motivating. Perhaps you can _______ them up?
    (A) cheer   (B) grow
    (C) gee   (D) throw

33. They're so miserable. Perhaps you can _______ them up?
    (A) cheer   (B) grow
    (C) put   (D) give

34. What's taking them so long? Perhaps you can _______ them up?
    (A) speak   (B) grow
    (C) give   (D) hurry

35. We can't hear you at the back. Perhaps you could _______ up a bit?
    (A) speak   (B) seize
    (C) put   (D) throw

—Darken Your Choice with HB Pencil—

1. Ⓐ Ⓑ Ⓒ Ⓓ	8. Ⓐ Ⓑ Ⓒ Ⓓ	15. Ⓐ Ⓑ Ⓒ Ⓓ	22 Ⓐ Ⓑ Ⓒ Ⓓ	29. Ⓐ Ⓑ Ⓒ Ⓓ
2. Ⓐ Ⓑ Ⓒ Ⓓ	9. Ⓐ Ⓑ Ⓒ Ⓓ	16. Ⓐ Ⓑ Ⓒ Ⓓ	23. Ⓐ Ⓑ Ⓒ Ⓓ	30. Ⓐ Ⓑ Ⓒ Ⓓ
3. Ⓐ Ⓑ Ⓒ Ⓓ	10. Ⓐ Ⓑ Ⓒ Ⓓ	17. Ⓐ Ⓑ Ⓒ Ⓓ	24. Ⓐ Ⓑ Ⓒ Ⓓ	31. Ⓐ Ⓑ Ⓒ Ⓓ
4. Ⓐ Ⓑ Ⓒ Ⓓ	11. Ⓐ Ⓑ Ⓒ Ⓓ	18. Ⓐ Ⓑ Ⓒ Ⓓ	25. Ⓐ Ⓑ Ⓒ Ⓓ	32. Ⓐ Ⓑ Ⓒ Ⓓ
5. Ⓐ Ⓑ Ⓒ Ⓓ	12. Ⓐ Ⓑ Ⓒ Ⓓ	19. Ⓐ Ⓑ Ⓒ Ⓓ	26. Ⓐ Ⓑ Ⓒ Ⓓ	33. Ⓐ Ⓑ Ⓒ Ⓓ
6. Ⓐ Ⓑ Ⓒ Ⓓ	13. Ⓐ Ⓑ Ⓒ Ⓓ	20. Ⓐ Ⓑ Ⓒ Ⓓ	27. Ⓐ Ⓑ Ⓒ Ⓓ	34. Ⓐ Ⓑ Ⓒ Ⓓ
7. Ⓐ Ⓑ Ⓒ Ⓓ	14. Ⓐ Ⓑ Ⓒ Ⓓ	21. Ⓐ Ⓑ Ⓒ Ⓓ	28. Ⓐ Ⓑ Ⓒ Ⓓ	35. Ⓐ Ⓑ Ⓒ Ⓓ

ADJECTIVES

LEARNING OBJECTIVES

- ➤ Adjectives of Quality
- ➤ Adjectives of Quantity

PRACTICE EXERCISE

I. Fill in the blanks with the correct option.

1. Generally, girls are _______ than boys.
   (A) talkative   (B) more talkative
   (C) most talkative   (D) none of these

2. Cricket is an _______ game.
   (A) exciting   (B) excitinger
   (C) excitengest   (D) none of these

3. Arpita is looking _______ in this dress.
   (A) gorgeous   (B) gorgeousest
   (C) gorgeouser   (D) none of these

4. She has a very _______ voice.
   (A) sour   (B) bitter
   (C) sweet   (D) none of these

5. Diamond is the _______ natural material.
   (A) hard   (B) harder
   (C) hardest   (D) none of these

6. This exercise is quite _______
   (A) more simple   (B) most simple
   (C) simple   (D) none of these

7. Rohan is a _______ boy.
   (A) trustworthy   (B) trustworthier
   (C) trustworthest   (D) none of these

8. The entire staff of the hotel we stayed at was very _______.
   (A) friendly   (B) friendlier
   (C) friendliest   (D) none of these

9. You are getting _______ all the time.
   (A) gooder   (B) goodest
   (C) better   (D) none of these

10. Your efforts to accomplish this project are _______.
    (A) outstandinger   (B) outstandingest
    (C) outstanding   (D) none of these

II. Fill in the blanks with the correct option.

11. My elder brother is 25, he still feels _______ when he sees cockroach.
    (A) frightender
    (B) frightened
    (C) frightendest
    (D) none of these

12. Mr. Sharma felt very _______ when his son failed the final examination.
    (A) more disappointed
    (B) most disappointed
    (C) disappointed
    (D) none of these

13. I feel _______ on Sundays.
    (A) relaxed   (B) relaxing
    (C) relaxful   (D) none of these

14. Rohan felt _______ when his manager shouted at him in front of his juniors.
    (A) proud   (B) honoured
    (C) ashamed   (D) none of these

15. He is ___________ so he avoids being photographed.
    (A) bashful   (B) confident
    (C) bold   (D) none of these
16. It is always ________to seek the advice of your elders in difficult times.
    (A) beneficial   (B) useless
    (C) necessity   (D) none of these
17. We had a ___________ time at the alumni meet.
    (A) least   (B) great
    (C) cool   (D) none of these
18. John is very _______ about his wedding.
    (A) excited   (B) boring
    (C) interesting   (D) None of these
19. He doesn't seem ____ in your offer.
    (A) interested
    (B) interesting
    (C) exciting
    (D) none of these
20. The news of her death _______ us.
    (A) stunning   (B) stunned
    (C) stunded   (D) none of these

HOTS (ACHIEVERS SECTION)

Read the passages that follow and choose the correct options that can replace the underlined portions.

Elephants are highly _____21_____ with relatively large, _____22_____ and _____23_____ brains. They have reasoning capabilities, can learn skills and have emotions experiencing pain, suffering, sadness and grief and they are even _____24_____ just like we are sometimes. They love to wallow in mud and swish their bodies with _____25_____ sand.

21. (A) agile   (B) lethargic
    (C) intelligent   (D) gigantic
22. (A) complex   (B) fast
    (C) simple   (D) uncomplicated
23. (A) quick-witted   (B) child-like
    (C) childish   (D) slow - maturing
24. (A) depressing   (B) mirthful
    (C) depressed   (D) caring
25. (A) rocky   (B) fluffy
    (C) grainy   (D) silken

—Darken Your Choice with HB Pencil—

1.	Ⓐ Ⓑ Ⓒ Ⓓ	6.	Ⓐ Ⓑ Ⓒ Ⓓ	11.	Ⓐ Ⓑ Ⓒ Ⓓ	16	Ⓐ Ⓑ Ⓒ Ⓓ	21.	Ⓐ Ⓑ Ⓒ Ⓓ
2.	Ⓐ Ⓑ Ⓒ Ⓓ	7.	Ⓐ Ⓑ Ⓒ Ⓓ	12.	Ⓐ Ⓑ Ⓒ Ⓓ	17.	Ⓐ Ⓑ Ⓒ Ⓓ	22.	Ⓐ Ⓑ Ⓒ Ⓓ
3.	Ⓐ Ⓑ Ⓒ Ⓓ	8.	Ⓐ Ⓑ Ⓒ Ⓓ	13.	Ⓐ Ⓑ Ⓒ Ⓓ	18.	Ⓐ Ⓑ Ⓒ Ⓓ	23.	Ⓐ Ⓑ Ⓒ Ⓓ
4.	Ⓐ Ⓑ Ⓒ Ⓓ	9.	Ⓐ Ⓑ Ⓒ Ⓓ	14.	Ⓐ Ⓑ Ⓒ Ⓓ	19.	Ⓐ Ⓑ Ⓒ Ⓓ	24.	Ⓐ Ⓑ Ⓒ Ⓓ
5.	Ⓐ Ⓑ Ⓒ Ⓓ	10.	Ⓐ Ⓑ Ⓒ Ⓓ	15.	Ⓐ Ⓑ Ⓒ Ⓓ	20.	Ⓐ Ⓑ Ⓒ Ⓓ	25.	Ⓐ Ⓑ Ⓒ Ⓓ

OLYMPIAD WORKBOOK (IEO) CLASS— 8

ARTICLES AND PREPOSITIONS

LEARNING OBJECTIVES

➤ Types of Articles

PRACTICE EXERCISE

I. Fill in the blanks with the most suitable article.

1. I want to buy ___________ laptop computer next week.
   (A) a   (B) an
   (C) the   (D) none of these

2. Can you please go to ___________ grocery store on Fifth Street and buy 2 cartons of milk?
   (A) a   (B) an
   (C) the   (D) none of these

3. Please meet me at the train station in ___________ hour from now.
   (A) a   (B) an
   (C) the   (D) none of these

4. I like to watch tennis on television. It is ___________ very good game.
   (A) a   (B) an
   (C) the   (D) none of these

5. My brother won an award for being ___________ best speller in our school.
   (A) a   (B) an
   (C) the   (D) none of these

6. I couldn't believe my eyes when I saw ___________ elephant crossing the road in front of my school yesterday.
   (A) a   (B) an
   (C) the   (D) none of these

7. Hello, my name is Bob! I have nothing to do tonight, so if you're not busy, would you like to watch ___________ movie or something with me?
   (A) a   (B) an
   (C) the   (D) none of these

8. How much will it cost to go on ___________ holiday to Bali?
   (A) a   (B) an
   (C) the   (D) none of these

9. Can you please help me pick out ___________ birthday present for my father?
   (A) a   (B) an
   (C) the   (D) none of these

10. ___________ President of the United States will be visiting Australia next week.
    (A) a   (B) an
    (C) the   (D) none of these

II. Fill in the blanks with a, an, the. Write (d) where no article is required.

11. I need ___________ egg for this recipe, but we're out.
    (A) an
    (B) a
    (C) the
    (D) none of these

12. I need __________ milk for this recipe, but we're out.
    (A) a   (B) an
    (C) the   (D) none of these
13. I need __________ potato for this recipe, but we're out.
    (A) an   (B) a
    (C) the   (D) no article
14. Is that __________ '8' or __________ 'B'? I can't read it.
    (A) a/an   (B) an/a
    (C) an/the   (D) no article
15. Is that __________ 'U' or __________ 'O'? I can't read it.
    (A) an/a   (B) a/the
    (C) a/an   (D) no article
16. He is from __________ European country, but I don't know which one.
    (A) a   (B) an
    (C) the   (D) no article
17. I enjoyed __________ DVD you gave me for my birthday.
    (A) the   (B) an
    (C) a   (D) no article
18. If I were rich, I would buy __________ apartment in Manhattan and   house in Hawaii.
    (A) an   (B) a
    (C) the   (D) no article
19. Do you know __________ name of her perfume?
    (A) a   (B) an
    (C) the   (D) no article
20. This school has __________ great teachers.
    (A) a   (B) an
    (C) the   (D) no article

III. Fill in the blanks with a suitable article. If no article is required, choose (d) no article.

21. I will give you _______ pen and _______ notebook.
    (A) a, an   (B) a, a
    (C) a, the   (D) no article

22. _______ house has windows.
    (A) An   (B) A
    (C) The   (D) No article
23. _______ house built of _______ stone is colder than one built of _______ brick.
    (A) A, no article, no article
    (B) An, a, no article
    (C) A, the, the
    (D) No article
24. You write on _______ blackboard with _______ chalk.
    (A) a, an   (B) a, the
    (C) a, no article   (D) no article
25. I want to listen to _______ music.
    (A) a   (B) an
    (C) the   (D) no article

IV. Choose the correct preposition to fill in the blanks.

26. You must be back _______ four o'clock.
    (A) in   (B) by
    (C) for   (D) to
27. Workout is necessary _______ health.
    (A) by
    (B) to
    (C) for
    (D) in
28. The Woman is looking _______ her diamond ring.
    (A) to
    (B) at
    (C) inside
    (D) in
29. The Woman is holding a cup of tea _______ her hands.
    (A) into
    (B) in
    (C) on
    (D) by
30. What are you doing _______ coming Sunday?
    (A) on   (B) in
    (C) to   (D) from

Choose the appropriate quantifier to complete the following sentences.

31. We have interviewed twenty candidates for the vacant position, but _______ of them was actually a good fit.
    (A) most   (B) neither
    (C) much   (D) none
    (E) no

32. Oakland is about to go bilingual, with two official languages, but _______ of them is English.
    (A) both   (B) none
    (C) neither   (D) either
    (E) no

33. On some computers there are keys which can have as many as five different functions _______.

    (A) either   (B) each
    (C) none   (D) every
    (E) both

34. _______ argument could move _______ man from this decision.
    (A) No / either   (B) Every / both
    (C) No / neither   (D) Each / all
    (E) Each / both

35. _______ Peter _______ Michael come here quite often but _______ of them gives us help.
    (A) Both / and / either
    (B) Neither / nor / both
    (C) Both / and / neither
    (D) Either / or / all
    (E) Both / or / any

—Darken Your Choice with HB Pencil—

1. Ⓐ Ⓑ Ⓒ Ⓓ	8. Ⓐ Ⓑ Ⓒ Ⓓ	15. Ⓐ Ⓑ Ⓒ Ⓓ	22 Ⓐ Ⓑ Ⓒ Ⓓ	29. Ⓐ Ⓑ Ⓒ Ⓓ
2. Ⓐ Ⓑ Ⓒ Ⓓ	9. Ⓐ Ⓑ Ⓒ Ⓓ	16. Ⓐ Ⓑ Ⓒ Ⓓ	23. Ⓐ Ⓑ Ⓒ Ⓓ	30. Ⓐ Ⓑ Ⓒ Ⓓ
3. Ⓐ Ⓑ Ⓒ Ⓓ	10. Ⓐ Ⓑ Ⓒ Ⓓ	17. Ⓐ Ⓑ Ⓒ Ⓓ	24. Ⓐ Ⓑ Ⓒ Ⓓ	31. Ⓐ Ⓑ Ⓒ Ⓓ
4. Ⓐ Ⓑ Ⓒ Ⓓ	11. Ⓐ Ⓑ Ⓒ Ⓓ	18. Ⓐ Ⓑ Ⓒ Ⓓ	25. Ⓐ Ⓑ Ⓒ Ⓓ	32. Ⓐ Ⓑ Ⓒ Ⓓ
5. Ⓐ Ⓑ Ⓒ Ⓓ	12. Ⓐ Ⓑ Ⓒ Ⓓ	19. Ⓐ Ⓑ Ⓒ Ⓓ	26. Ⓐ Ⓑ Ⓒ Ⓓ	33. Ⓐ Ⓑ Ⓒ Ⓓ
6. Ⓐ Ⓑ Ⓒ Ⓓ	13. Ⓐ Ⓑ Ⓒ Ⓓ	20. Ⓐ Ⓑ Ⓒ Ⓓ	27. Ⓐ Ⓑ Ⓒ Ⓓ	34. Ⓐ Ⓑ Ⓒ Ⓓ
7. Ⓐ Ⓑ Ⓒ Ⓓ	14. Ⓐ Ⓑ Ⓒ Ⓓ	21. Ⓐ Ⓑ Ⓒ Ⓓ	28. Ⓐ Ⓑ Ⓒ Ⓓ	35. Ⓐ Ⓑ Ⓒ Ⓓ

CONJUNCTIONS AND DETERMINERS

LEARNING OBJECTIVES

➤ Conjunctions
➤ Determiners

PRACTICE EXERCISE

1. Fill in the blanks with the most appropriate conjunctions:

   _______ Kanu or her brother has won the trophy.
   (A) Neither   (B) Either
   (C) When   (D) So

2. Fill in the blanks with the most appropriate conjunctions:

   The principal _______ the staff encouraged the hockey players.
   (A) but   (B) as well as
   (C) as soon as   (D) nor

3. Fill in the blanks with the most appropriate conjunctions:

   I don't know whether he appeared in the test _______ not.
   (A) or   (B) nor
   (C) that   (D) and

4. Fill in the blanks with the most appropriate conjunctions:

   _______ you practice hard, you can't win the boxing title.
   (A) Until   (B) Till
   (C) Unless   (D) If

5. Fill in the blanks with the most appropriate conjunctions:

   Raju relishes not only Chinese _______ continental food.

   (A) also   (B) but
   (C) but also   (D) rather

6. Fill in the blanks with the most appropriate conjunctions:

   Sonali prepares delicious food _______ she does not garnish it well.
   (A) and   (B) but
   (C) but also   (D) also

7. Fill in the blanks with the most appropriate conjunctions:

   No sooner did the mariner set the sails _______ it began to rain.
   (A) then   (B) than
   (C) when   (D) after

8. Fill in the blanks with the most appropriate conjunctions:

   Hardly had the child seen the mother _______ he came running towards her.
   (A) then   (B) than
   (C) when   (D) as

9. Fill in the blanks with the most appropriate conjunctions:

   _______ he switched on the machine, the power went off.
   (A) As soon as   (B) Such as
   (C) Then   (D) As well as

10. Fill in the blanks with the most appropriate conjunctions:

_______our friends are in trouble, we must help them.
(A) As soon as
(B) As
(C) Than
(D) But

11. Fill in the blanks with the most appropriate conjunctions:

After failure, Aman did nothing else _______ weep.
(A) than
(B) then
(C) when
(D) but

12. Fill in the blanks with the most appropriate determiners:

In _______ countries, medical treatment is free of cost.
(A) a lot of
(B) whole
(C) many
(D) none of these

13. Fill in the blanks with the most appropriate determiners:

_______ people think that modernization is another name for development.
(A) A lot many
(B) A lot of
(C) A little few
(D) None of these

14. Fill in the blanks with the most appropriate determiners:

Only _______ houses were not damaged by the earthquake.
(A) a little
(B) much
(C) a few
(D) none of these

15. Fill in the blanks with the most appropriate determiners:

You must learn _______ English every day to improve it.
(A) a few
(B) a little
(C) a lot of
(D) none of these

16. Fill in the blanks with the most appropriate determiners:

_______ plates and glasses are usually broken in a party.
(A) Any
(B) A little
(C) Some
(D) None of these

17. Fill in the blanks with the most appropriate determiners:

There isn't _______ bread in the refrigerator.
(A) any
(B) some
(C) each
(D) none of these

18. Fill in the blanks with the most appropriate determiners:

We expect _______ man to do his best.
(A) every
(B) whole
(C) less
(D) some

19. Fill in the blanks with the most appropriate determiners:

I have _______friends in London.
(A) each
(B) a few
(C) much
(D) all

20. Fill in the blanks with the most appropriate determiners:

_______ knowledge is a dangerous thing.
(A) Few
(B) A little
(C) Some
(D) Any

21. Fill in the blanks with the correct options.

    Together, Ali _______ Ahmed will compete in the race.

    (A) but   (B) with

    (C) And   (D) yet

22. Fill in the blanks with the correct options.

    _______ you do anything else, clear up this mess first.

    (A) Before   (B) After

    (C) While   (D) Unless

23. Fill in the blanks with the correct options.

    Elephants like to eat leaves ____ they are herbivorous.

    (A) Although   (B) yet

    (C) Unless   (D) since

24. Fill in the blanks with the correct options.

    The baby falls asleep _______ her mother sings her a lullaby.

    (A) Unless   (B) until

    (C) Whenever   (D) although

25. Fill in the blanks with the correct options.

    Our school choir sang the school song ____ the school flag was raised.

    (A) Before   (B) as

    (C) Throughout   (D) Until

Darken Your Choice with HB Pencil

1. Ⓐ Ⓑ Ⓒ Ⓓ	6. Ⓐ Ⓑ Ⓒ Ⓓ	11. Ⓐ Ⓑ Ⓒ Ⓓ	16. Ⓐ Ⓑ Ⓒ Ⓓ	21. Ⓐ Ⓑ Ⓒ Ⓓ
2. Ⓐ Ⓑ Ⓒ Ⓓ	7. Ⓐ Ⓑ Ⓒ Ⓓ	12. Ⓐ Ⓑ Ⓒ Ⓓ	17. Ⓐ Ⓑ Ⓒ Ⓓ	22. Ⓐ Ⓑ Ⓒ Ⓓ
3. Ⓐ Ⓑ Ⓒ Ⓓ	8. Ⓐ Ⓑ Ⓒ Ⓓ	13. Ⓐ Ⓑ Ⓒ Ⓓ	18. Ⓐ Ⓑ Ⓒ Ⓓ	23. Ⓐ Ⓑ Ⓒ Ⓓ
4. Ⓐ Ⓑ Ⓒ Ⓓ	9. Ⓐ Ⓑ Ⓒ Ⓓ	14. Ⓐ Ⓑ Ⓒ Ⓓ	19. Ⓐ Ⓑ Ⓒ Ⓓ	24. Ⓐ Ⓑ Ⓒ Ⓓ
5. Ⓐ Ⓑ Ⓒ Ⓓ	10. Ⓐ Ⓑ Ⓒ Ⓓ	15. Ⓐ Ⓑ Ⓒ Ⓓ	20. Ⓐ Ⓑ Ⓒ Ⓓ	25. Ⓐ Ⓑ Ⓒ Ⓓ

JUMBLED WORDS 

➤ Jumbled words
➤ Jumbled sentences

PRACTICE EXERCISE

1. Choose the correct order of the words/ phrases out of the given options to make a meaningful sentence.

   I/?/off/see/come/the/airport/at/can/ to/you

   (A) To see you off at the airport can I come?

   (B) I can come to see you off at the airport?

   (C) Can I come to see you off at the airport?

   (D) None of the above

2. Choose the correct order of the words/ phrases out of the given options to make a meaningful sentence.

   who/god/are/those/do not/atheists/ believe/in

   (A) Atheists are called those who do not believe in God.

   (B) Those who do not believe in God are called atheists.

   (C) Those are called atheists who do not believe in God.

   (D) None of the above

3. Choose the correct order of the words/ phrases out of the given options to make a meaningful sentence.

   harmless/most/humans/to/bats/are

   (A) Harmless are most bats to humans.

   (B) Humans are harmless to most bats.

   (C) Most bats are harmless to humans.

   (D) None of the above

4. Choose the correct order of the words/ phrases out of the given options to make a meaningful sentence.

   has/cancelled/doctor's/of/unavailabil- ity/the/appointment/got/because/the

   (A) The appointment has got cancelled because of the doctor's unavailability.

   (B) The appointment has got cancelled because of unavailability the doctor's.

   (C) Because of the unavailability doctor's the appointment has got cancelled.

   (D) None of the above

5. Choose the correct order of the words/ phrases out of the given options to make a meaningful sentence.

   plays/role/everyone's/music/an/in/ life/important

   (A) An important role in everyone's life music plays.

   (B) In everyone's life plays an important role music.

   (C) Music plays an important role in everyone's life.

   (D) None of the above

6. Choose the correct order of the words/ phrases out of the given options to make a meaningful sentence.

John and Samantha/last Sunday/went/ to church

(A) Samantha and John last Sunday went to church.
(B) John and Samantha went to church last Sunday.
(C) Went to church last Sunday John and Samantha.
(D) None of the above

7. Choose the correct order of the words/ phrases out of the given options to make a meaningful sentence.

living/dreams/Jenny/in/France

(A) Dreams of living in France Jenny.
(B) Jenny dreams of living in France.
(C) France of living dreams Jenny.
(D) None of the above

8. Choose the correct order of the words/ phrases out of the given options to make a meaningful sentence.

summer holiday's/start/to/can't wait/I/ for/my

(A) I can't wait for my summer holidays to start.
(B) To start I can't wait for my summer holidays.
(C) Summer holidays for I can't wait to start my.
(D) None of the above

9. Choose the correct order of the words/ phrases out of the given options to make a meaningful sentence.

give/intelligence/norms/age/each/ tests/the/of

(A) Intelligence tests give the norms of each age.
(B) Give the norms of each age intelligence tests.
(C) Each age give the norms of intelligence tests.
(D) None of the above

10. Choose the correct order of the words/ phrases out of the given options to make a meaningful sentence.

the basic information/to be culturally literate/to thrive/is to posses the/in the modern world

(A) The basic information needed to thrive in the modern world to be culturally literate is to possess.
(B) To possess the basic informations to be culturally literate is needed to thrive in the modern world.
(C) To be culturally literate is to posses the basic information needed to thrive in the modern world.
(D) None of the above

11. Choose the correct order of the words/ phrases out of the given options to make a meaningful sentence.

that/deserts/and/scorpions/live/ tropical/nocturnal/areas/are/animals/ in

(A) Scorpions are nocturnal animals that live in tropical areas and deserts.
(B) In tropical areas and deserts scorpions are nocturnal animals that live.
(C) Scorpions live in tropical areas and deserts that are nocturnal animals.
(D) None of the above

12. Choose the correct order of the words/ phrases out of the given options to make a meaningful sentence.

persons/of different/meet/nationalities/ on/common ground/a

(A) Persons of different nationalities on a common ground meet.
(B) On a common ground persons of different nationalities meet.
(C) Persons of different nationalities meet on a common ground.
(D) None of the above

13. Choose the correct order of the words/ phrases out of the given options to make a meaningful sentence.

has/vegetable soup/my doctor/recommended/only

(A) Vegetable soup has recommended only my doctor.
(B) My doctor has recommended only vegetable soup.
(C) Has recommended vegetable soup only my doctor.
(D) None of the above

14. Choose the correct order of the words/ phrases out of the given options to make a meaningful sentence.

nervous system/due to/extensive damage/is possible

(A) Extensive damage is possible due to nervous system.
(B) Due to nervous system extensive damage is possible.
(C) Is possible due to nervous system extensive damage.
(D) None of the above

15. Choose the correct order of the words/ phrases out of the given options to make a meaningful sentence.

before/my/crashed/got/the/meeting/ system/just

(A) My system just before the meeting got crashed.
(B) Just before the meeting my system got crashed.
(C) My system got crashed just before the meeting.
(D) None of the above

16. Choose the correct order of the words/ phrases out of the given options to make a meaningful sentence.

Large quantities/of warm water/ drinking/results/in/sweating

(A) Drinking of warm water results in sweating a large quantities.
(B) Drinking large quantities of warm water results in sweating.
(C) Drinking of large quantities warm water results in sweating.
(D) None of the above

17. Choose the correct order of the words/ phrases out of the given options to make a meaningful sentence.

the/lighten/good/of/home/in/every/ books/knowledge/up/lamp

(A) Lighten up the lamp of knowledge good books in every home.
(B) Good books lighten up the lamp of knowledge in every home.
(C) The lamp of knowledge in every home good books lighten up.
(D) None of the above

18. Choose the correct order of the words/ phrases out of the given options to make a meaningful sentence.

Many cooks/spoil/too many/broth

(A) Too many cooks spoil the broth.
(B) Many cooks too spoil the broth.
(C) Spoil the broth too many cooks.
(D) None of the above

19. Choose the correct order of the words/ phrases out of the given options to make a meaningful sentence.

comprehension/is/high/her/language/ is/of/very

(A) Comprehension of language her is very high.
(B) Her is very high of language comprehension.
(C) Her comprehension of language is very high.
(D) None of the above

20. Choose the correct order of the words/ phrases out of the given options to make a meaningful sentence.

can't/I/the/attend/function/I/am/ week/next/afraid

(A) Afraid I am I can't attend the function next week.
(B) I can't attend the function next week I am afraid.
(C) I am afraid I can't attend the function next week.
(D) None of the above

Choose the correct order of the words out of the given options to make a meaningful sentence.

21. I / have / risk / taken / saving / her / a / in / great.
    (A) I taken have a great risk in saving her.
    (B) A great risk have I taken in saving her.
    (C) Her have taken I a great risk in saving.
    (D) I have taken a great risk in saving her.

22. the road / of / obey / we / rules / the / must.
    (A) The rules of the road must we obey.
    (B) We obey the must rules of the road.
    (C) We must obey the rules of the road.
    (D) We must obey the road of the rules.

23. storm / clouds / the / seen / were / dark / before.
    (A) Storm were seen before the dark clouds.
    (B) Dark clouds were seen before the storm.
    (C) Dark clouds were seen the before storm.
    (D) The storm before the dark clouds were seen.

24. in studies / he is / in games / and / good / both.
    (A) He is both good in studies and in games.
    (B) He is both good in and studies games.
    (C) He is good in both studies and games.
    (D) He is good both in studies and in games.

25. the teachers / a / is / favourite / of all / Ramesh.
    (A) Ramesh is a favourite of all the teachers.
    (B) Ramesh the teachers is favourite of all.
    (C) All the teachers is favourite of Ramesh.
    (D) Ramesh is a favourite of the all teachers.

1.	A B C D	6.	A B C D	11.	A B C D	16	A B C D	21.	A B C D
2.	A B C D	7.	A B C D	12.	A B C D	17.	A B C D	22.	A B C D
3.	A B C D	8.	A B C D	13.	A B C D	18.	A B C D	23.	A B C D
4.	A B C D	9.	A B C D	14.	A B C D	19.	A B C D	24.	A B C D
5.	A B C D	10.	A B C D	15.	A B C D	20.	A B C D	25.	A B C D

TENSES

➤ Basic concepts of Tenses
➤ Different types of Tenses
➤ Concept of Conditional Sentences

PRACTICE EXERCISE

I. Choose the correct option to complete the following sentences.

1. I ___________ for them for an hour now. I can't wait any longer.
   (A) wait
   (B) am waiting
   (C) have been waiting
   (D) none of these

2. I hope __________ some interesting read in the new bookshop.
   (A) to find   (B) find
   (C) found   (D) none of these

3. Jane __________ TV for hours; that's why her eyes are red.
   (A) is watching
   (B) watch
   (C) has been watching
   (D) none of these

4. Unless John __________ harder, he won't get this job.
   (A) tried   (B) will try
   (C) tries   (D) none of these

5. Stop __________ that terrible noise.
   (A) making   (B) make
   (C) made   (D) none of these

6. He will see you as soon as Mr. Brown ___________.
   (A) leaves   (B) will leave
   (C) left   (D) none of these

7. I realized that my parents __________ me and my brother.
   (A) have adopted   (B) had adopted

8. No one __________ text to me like that.
   (A) has ever spoken
   (B) ever spoke

9. We normally live with our parents but for these two months we __________ in our aunt's flat.
   (A) live   (B) are living

10. We __________ to the theatre tonight.
    (A) go   (B) are going

II. Choose the correct option to fill in the blanks with the correct form of the verbs given in brackets.

11. Next week we __________ into our new house. (move)
    (A) will move   (B) had move
    (C) do move   (D) moved

12. He was sure that he __________ that man before. (see)
    (A) will see   (B) had seen
    (C) has seen   (D) seen

13. What ___________ have for breakfast?
(you, have)
(A) will you   (B) do you
(C) did you   (D) are you

14. She ___________ a bath when the telephone ___________ (have, ring).
(A) will have, rang
(B) is having, rang
(C) was having, rang
(D) were having, rang

15. She ___________ the piano for eight years. (play)
(A) will play   (B) play
(C) have played   (D) played

16. He ___________ never on time. (be)
(A) is   (B) are
(C) did   (D) am

17. You look terrible. ___________ (you, drink) ?
(A) do you drink   (B) did you drink
(C) have you drunk   (D) will you drink

18. He realized that he ___________ his keys. (lose)
(A) has lost   (B) have lost
(C) had lost   (D) lost

19. I ___________ very angry with you if you do not stop smoking. (be)
(A) will be   (B) had been
(C) do be   (D) should be

20. They ___________ for her for some time when she finally ___________ (wait, arrive).
(A) had, arrived
(B) had arrived, lost
(C) have been waiting, arrived
(D) had been waiting, arrived

III. Choose the most suitable option to fill in the blanks.

21. Two children and one adult ___________ in a fire last night.
(A) died   (B) have died
(C) are dying   (D) will die

22. Sam ___________ the marathon for the first time in 2009.
(A) has run   (B) runs
(C) ran   (D) is running

23. I ___________ English tea. Is it good?
(A) drink
(B) 've never drunk
(C) have drunk
(D) am drinking

24. We ___________ Mrs. Stewart when we were in California.
(A) will meet   (B) are meeting
(C) met   (D) have met

25. He's not happy because his brother ___________ his computer.
(A) doesn't use   (B) using
(C) has used   (D) will use

26. If it's sunny tomorrow, maybe we ___________ go to the beach.
(A) went   (B) will go
(C) don't go   (D) go

27. I ___________ my exercise because I didn't understand the questions.
(A) didn't do   (B) will do
(C) did   (D) won't do

28. She ___________ the piano very well.
(A) play   (B) playing
(C) will play   (D) plays

29. My brother ___________ football in the same club as me.
(A) play   (B) plays
(C) is playing   (D) played

30. I ___________ in a first-class hotel: it's too expensive for me.
(A) 'm going to sleep
(B) 've never slept
(C) sleep
(D) am sleeping

Fill in the blanks with the correct tense form of the verbs given in brackets.

31. I (have) ___________ the same car for more than ten years. I'm thinking about buying a new one.

32. I (love) ___________ chocolate since I was a child. You might even call me a "chocoholic."

33. Lately, I (think) ___________ about changing my career because I (become) ___________ dissatisfied with the conditions at my company.

34. John (work) ___________ for the government since he graduated from Harvard University. Until recently, he (enjoy) ___________ his work, but now he is talking about retiring.

35. How long (be) ___________ in Canada?

---Darken Your Choice with HB Pencil---

1.	Ⓐ Ⓑ Ⓒ Ⓓ	8.	Ⓐ Ⓑ Ⓒ Ⓓ	15.	Ⓐ Ⓑ Ⓒ Ⓓ	22	Ⓐ Ⓑ Ⓒ Ⓓ	29.	Ⓐ Ⓑ Ⓒ Ⓓ
2.	Ⓐ Ⓑ Ⓒ Ⓓ	9.	Ⓐ Ⓑ Ⓒ Ⓓ	16.	Ⓐ Ⓑ Ⓒ Ⓓ	23.	Ⓐ Ⓑ Ⓒ Ⓓ	30.	Ⓐ Ⓑ Ⓒ Ⓓ
3.	Ⓐ Ⓑ Ⓒ Ⓓ	10.	Ⓐ Ⓑ Ⓒ Ⓓ	17.	Ⓐ Ⓑ Ⓒ Ⓓ	24.	Ⓐ Ⓑ Ⓒ Ⓓ	31.	Ⓐ Ⓑ Ⓒ Ⓓ
4.	Ⓐ Ⓑ Ⓒ Ⓓ	11.	Ⓐ Ⓑ Ⓒ Ⓓ	18.	Ⓐ Ⓑ Ⓒ Ⓓ	25.	Ⓐ Ⓑ Ⓒ Ⓓ	32.	Ⓐ Ⓑ Ⓒ Ⓓ
5.	Ⓐ Ⓑ Ⓒ Ⓓ	12.	Ⓐ Ⓑ Ⓒ Ⓓ	19.	Ⓐ Ⓑ Ⓒ Ⓓ	26.	Ⓐ Ⓑ Ⓒ Ⓓ	33.	Ⓐ Ⓑ Ⓒ Ⓓ
6.	Ⓐ Ⓑ Ⓒ Ⓓ	13.	Ⓐ Ⓑ Ⓒ Ⓓ	20.	Ⓐ Ⓑ Ⓒ Ⓓ	27.	Ⓐ Ⓑ Ⓒ Ⓓ	34.	Ⓐ Ⓑ Ⓒ Ⓓ
7.	Ⓐ Ⓑ Ⓒ Ⓓ	14.	Ⓐ Ⓑ Ⓒ Ⓓ	21.	Ⓐ Ⓑ Ⓒ Ⓓ	28.	Ⓐ Ⓑ Ⓒ Ⓓ	35.	Ⓐ Ⓑ Ⓒ Ⓓ

VOICES AND NARRATION

LEARNING OBJECTIVES

➤ Voice and its two different types – Active and Passive

PRACTICE EXERCISE

I. Fill in the blanks with suitable active and passive form of verb.

1. This house _____________ in 1970 by my grandfather.
   (A) built
   (B) was built
   (C) was build
   (D) has built

2. The robbers _____________ by the police.
   (A) have arrested
   (B) have been arrested
   (C) was arrested
   (D) had arrested

3. We _____________ for the examination.
   (A) have preparing
   (B) are preparing
   (C) had preparing
   (D) have been prepared

4. It _____________ since yesterday.
   (A) is raining
   (B) has been raining
   (C) have been raining
   (D) was raining

5. I _____________ for five hours.
   (A) have been working
   (B) has been working
   (C) was working
   (D) am working

6. The students _____________ to submit their reports by the end of this week.
   (A) have asked
   (B) are asked
   (C) has asked
   (D) are asking

7. She _____________ for a while.
   (A) are ailing
   (B) is ailing
   (C) has been ailing
   (D) have been ailing

8. The teacher _____________ the student for lying.
   (A) has been punished
   (B) punished
   (C) is punished
   (D) was punished

9. I _____________ to become a successful writer.
   (A) have always wanted
   (B) am always wanted
   (C) was always wanted
   (D) am always wanting

10. The inmates of the juvenile home _____________ well by their caretakers.
    (A) were not being treated
    (B) were not treating
    (C) have not being treated
    (D) was not being treated

OLYMPIAD WORKBOOK (IEO) CLASS – 8

II. From the given alternatives, choose the one which best expresses the given sentence in Passive/Active voice.

11. They have built a perfect dam across the river.
    (A) Across the river a perfect dam was built.
    (B) A perfect dam has been built across the river by them.
    (C) A perfect dam should have been built by them.
    (D) Across the river was a perfect dam.

12. Do you imitate others?
    (A) Are others being imitated by you?
    (B) Are others imitated by you?
    (C) Have others being imitated by you?
    (D) Were others being imitated by you?

13. You need to clean your shoes properly.
    (A) Your shoes are needed to clean properly.
    (B) You are needed to clean your shoes properly.
    (C) Your shoes need to be cleaned properly by you.
    (D) Your shoes are needed by you to clean properly.

14. He is said to be very rich.
    (A) He said he is very rich.
    (B) People say he is very rich.
    (C) He said it is very rich.
    (D) People say it is very rich.

15. The invigilator was reading out the instructions.
    (A) The instructions were read by the invigilator.
    (B) The instructions were being read out by the invigilator.
    (C) The instructions had been read out by the invigilator.
    (D) The instructions had been read by the invigilator.

III. Choose the correct option to fill in the blanks.

16. Over a million dollars in cash __________ from the Bank of East Asia in Central.
    (A) have stolen
    (B) have been stolen
    (C) had stolen
    (D) been stolen

17. Thieves __________ over a million dollars in cash from the Bank of East Asia in Central.
    (A) stolen
    (B) were stolen
    (C) have stolen
    (D) was been stolen

18. I'll have to come by bus as my car _______ .
    (A) is repairing
    (B) is being repaired
    (C) repaired
    (D) been repaired

19. The gold __________ in a cave near the top of the mountain.
    (A) was discovered
    (B) discovered
    (C) been discovered
    (B) had discovered

20. Archaeologists __________ the gold in a cave near the top of the mountain.
    (A) were discovered
    (B) was discovered
    (C) discovered
    (D) none of these

IV. Choose the correct option from the choices given below.

21. Mary "I love chocolate."
    Jill: "Mary said (that) she ___ chocolate."
    (A) loved
    (B) loves
    (C) loving
    (D) none of these

22. Mary: "I went skiing."
    Jill: "Mary said (that) she ___ skiing."
    (A) went   (B) had gone
    (C) have gone   (D) none of these

23. Mary: "I will eat steak for dinner."
Jill: "Mary said (that) she ___ eat steak for dinner."
(A) willing
(B) will
(C) would
(D) none of these

24. Mary: "I have been to Sydney."
Jill: "Mary said (that) she ___ to Sydney."
(A) had been
(B) has been
(C) was being
(D) none of these

25. Mary: "I have had three cars."
Jill: "Mary said (that) she ___ three cars.
(A) has
(B) has had
(C) had had
(D) none of these

V. Select the most appropriate option to fill in the blanks.

26. I told him ___ do it.
(A) to not
(B) to don't
(C) not to
(D) don't

27. He asked us ___ show our passports.
(A) if
(B) to
(C) for
(D) that

28. She asked us if we ___ finished the work on Monday.
(A) have
(B) had
(C) either could be used here
(D) none of these

29. She asked us ___ on time.
(A) to be
(B) for being
(C) been
(D) being

30. She asked if she ___ leave early.
(A) can
(B) could
(C) may
(D) must

HOTS (ACHIEVERS SECTION)

I. Choose the option which best expresses the given sentence in Indirect/Direct speech.

31. The boy said, "Who dare call you a thief?"
(A) The boy enquired who dared call him a thief.
(B) The boy asked who called him a thief.
(C) The boy told that who dared call him a thief.
(D) The boy wondered who dared call a thief.

32. She exclaimed with sorrow that it was a very miserable plight.
(A) She said with sorrow, "What a pity it is."
(B) She said, "What a mystery it is."
(C) She said, "What a miserable sight it is."
(D) She said, "What a miserable plight it is."

33. Dhruv said that he was sick and tired of working for that company.
(A) Dhruv said, "I am sick and tired of working for this company."
(B) Dhruv said, "He was tired of that company."
(C) Dhruv said to me, "I am sick and tired of working for this company."
(D) Dhruv said, "I will be tired of working for that company."

34. "Are you alone, my son?" asked a soft voice close behind me.
(A) A soft voice asked that what I was doing there alone.
(B) A soft voice said to me are you alone son.
(C) A soft voice from my back asked if I was alone.
(D) A soft voice behind me asked if I was alone.

35. She said to him, "Why don't you go today?"
    (A) She asked him why he did not go that day.
    (B) She said to him why he don't go that day.
    (C) She asked him not to go that day.
    (D) She asked him why he did not go today

1.	Ⓐ Ⓑ Ⓒ Ⓓ	8.	Ⓐ Ⓑ Ⓒ Ⓓ	15.	Ⓐ Ⓑ Ⓒ Ⓓ	22	Ⓐ Ⓑ Ⓒ Ⓓ	29.	Ⓐ Ⓑ Ⓒ Ⓓ
2.	Ⓐ Ⓑ Ⓒ Ⓓ	9.	Ⓐ Ⓑ Ⓒ Ⓓ	16.	Ⓐ Ⓑ Ⓒ Ⓓ	23.	Ⓐ Ⓑ Ⓒ Ⓓ	30.	Ⓐ Ⓑ Ⓒ Ⓓ
3.	Ⓐ Ⓑ Ⓒ Ⓓ	10.	Ⓐ Ⓑ Ⓒ Ⓓ	17.	Ⓐ Ⓑ Ⓒ Ⓓ	24.	Ⓐ Ⓑ Ⓒ Ⓓ	31.	Ⓐ Ⓑ Ⓒ Ⓓ
4.	Ⓐ Ⓑ Ⓒ Ⓓ	11.	Ⓐ Ⓑ Ⓒ Ⓓ	18.	Ⓐ Ⓑ Ⓒ Ⓓ	25.	Ⓐ Ⓑ Ⓒ Ⓓ	32.	Ⓐ Ⓑ Ⓒ Ⓓ
5.	Ⓐ Ⓑ Ⓒ Ⓓ	12.	Ⓐ Ⓑ Ⓒ Ⓓ	19.	Ⓐ Ⓑ Ⓒ Ⓓ	26.	Ⓐ Ⓑ Ⓒ Ⓓ	33.	Ⓐ Ⓑ Ⓒ Ⓓ
6.	Ⓐ Ⓑ Ⓒ Ⓓ	13.	Ⓐ Ⓑ Ⓒ Ⓓ	20.	Ⓐ Ⓑ Ⓒ Ⓓ	27.	Ⓐ Ⓑ Ⓒ Ⓓ	34.	Ⓐ Ⓑ Ⓒ Ⓓ
7.	Ⓐ Ⓑ Ⓒ Ⓓ	14.	Ⓐ Ⓑ Ⓒ Ⓓ	21.	Ⓐ Ⓑ Ⓒ Ⓓ	28.	Ⓐ Ⓑ Ⓒ Ⓓ	35.	Ⓐ Ⓑ Ⓒ Ⓓ

VOICES AND NARRATION

PRACTICE EXERCISE

I. Read the passage and answer the questions that follow.

The name of Florence Nightingale lives in the memory of the world by virtue of the heroic adventure of the Crimea. Had she died - as she nearly did - upon her return to England, her reputation would hardly have been different; her legend would have come down to us almost as we know it today - that gentle vision of female virtue which first took shape before the adoring eyes of the sick soldiers at Scutari. Yet, as a matter of fact, she lived for more than half a century after the Crimean War; and during the greater part of that long period all the energy and all the devotion of her extraordinary nature were working at their highest pitch. What she accomplished in those years of unknown labor could, indeed, hardly have been more glorious than her Crimean triumphs; but it was certainly more important. The true history was far stranger even than the myth. In Miss Nightingale's own eyes the adventure of the Crimea was a mere incident - scarcely more than a useful stepping-stone in her career. It was the fulcrum with which she hoped to move the world; but it was only the fulcrum. For more than a generation she was to sit in secret, working her lever: and her real life began at the very moment when, in popular imagination, it had ended.

She arrived in England in a shattered state of health. The hardships and the ceaseless efforts of the last two years had undermined her nervous system; her heart was affected; she suffered constantly from fainting-fits and terrible attacks of utter physical prostration. The doctors declared that one thing alone would save her - a complete and prolonged rest. But that was also the one thing with which she would have nothing to do. She had never been in the habit of resting; why should she begin now? Now, when her opportunity had come at last; now, when the iron was hot, and it was time to strike? No; she had work to do; and, come what might, she would do it. The doctors protested in vain; in vain her family lamented and entreated, in vain her friends pointed out to her the madness of such a course. Madness? Mad - possessed - perhaps she was. A frenzy had seized upon her. As she lay upon her sofa, gasping, she devoured blue-books, dictated letters, and, in the intervals of her palpitations, cracked jokes. For months at a stretch she never left her bed. But she would not rest. At this rate, the doctors assured her, even if she did not die, she would become an invalid for life. She could not help that; there was work to be done; and, as for rest, very likely she might rest ... when she had done it.

Wherever she went, to London or in the country, in the hills of Derbyshire, or among the rhododendrons at Embley, she was haunted by a ghost. It was the specter of Scutari - the hideous vision of the organization of a military hospital. She would lay that phantom, or she would perish. The whole system of the Army Medical Department, the education of the Medical Officer, the regulations of hospital procedure ... rest? How could she rest while these things were as they were, while, if the like necessity were to arise again, the like results would follow? And, even in peace and at home, what was the sanitary condition of the Army? The mortality in the barracks, was, she found, nearly double the mortality in civil life. 'You might as well take 1,100 men every year out upon Salisbury Plain and shoot them,' she said. After inspecting the hospitals at Chatham, she smiled grimly. 'Yes, this is one more symptom of the system which, in the Crimea, put to death 16,000 men.' Scutari had given her knowledge; and it had given her power too: her enormous reputation was at her back - an incalculable force. Other work, other duties, might lie before her; but the most urgent, the most obvious, of all was to look to the health of the Army.

Adapted from: Eminent Victorians, Lytton Strachey (1918)

1. According to the author, the work done during the last fifty years of Florence Nightingale's life was, when compared with her work in the Crimea, all of the following except
   (A) less dramatic
   (B) less demanding
   (C) less well-known to the public
   (D) more important
   (E) more rewarding to Miss Nightingale herself.

2. The 'fulcrum' (para 1) refers to her
   (A) reputation
   (B) mental energy
   (C) physical energy
   (D) overseas contacts
   (E) commitment to a cause

3. Paragraph 2 paints a picture of a woman who is.
   (A) an incapacitated invalid
   (B) mentally shattered
   (C) stubborn and querulous
   (D) physically weak but mentally indomitable
   (E) purposeful yet tiresome

4. The primary purpose of paragraph 3 is to.
   (A) account for conditions in the army
   (B) show the need for hospital reform
   (C) explain Miss Nightingale's main concerns
   (D) argue that peacetime conditions were worse than wartime conditions
   (E) delineate Miss Nightingale's plan for reform

5. The series of questions in paragraphs 2 and 3 are.
   (A) the author's attempt to show the thoughts running through Miss Nightingale's mind
   (B) Miss Nightingale questioning her own conscience
   (C) Miss Nightingale's response to an actual questioner
   (D) Responses to the doctors who advised rest
   (E) The author's device to highlight the reactions to Miss Nightingale's plans

6. The author's attitude to his material is.
   (A) disinterested reporting of biographical details
   (B) over-inflation of a reputation
   (C) debunking a myth
   (D) uncritical presentation of facts
   (E) interpretation as well as narration

7. In her statement, Miss Nightingale intended to.
   (A) criticize the conditions in hospitals
   (B) highlight the unhealthy conditions under which ordinary soldiers were living
   (C) prove that conditions in the barracks were as bad as those in a military hospital
   (D) ridicule the dangers of army life

(E) quote important statistics

II. Read the passage and answer the questions that follow.

14-lane, 7500 Crore Delhi-Meerut Express-way Launched By PM Modi December 31, 2015 14:33 IST NOIDA: Prime Minister Narendra Modi on Thursday launched a Rs. 7500 Crore project to widen the Delhi-Meerut highway and replace it with an expressway to decongest Delhi. He described it as the "road to freedom from pollution." The road connecting Meerut to Delhi is the busiest highway in the region, Union minister Nitin Gadkari said minutes before the prime minister spoke. The expressway will do away with 31 traffic signals on the road and make it "signal free", reducing travel time between Meerut and Delhi from two and a half hours to around 40 minutes, he said. "This highway will show the path to tackle pollution," PM Modi said. Delhi is the most polluted capital in the world." In the changing times, pace will not slacken. It will only get faster," he said. Mr Modi said his government will take forward the programmes started by the Atal Bihari Vajpayee government. "Vajpayee ji had two projects - the Golden quadrilateral connecting four corners of the country and he started a programme to give connectivity to villages," he said referring to the Prime Minister Rural Roads Programme. Even the villagers now are not satisfied with single lane roads. They want double lane and four lane roads. Every villager understands that if his village has to be connected to the path of development, his village must be connected to the highway," PM Modi said.

8. Which project has been launched by PM Modi?

9. In how many phases the project will be launched?

10. How much time will the new road save after it is ready to use?

11. How many projects did Mr Atal Bihari Vajpayee ji launch?

12. What is the total cost of the project?

HOTS (ACHIEVERS SECTION)

Read the passage and answer the questions accordingly.

SEAT BELTS

"Click!" That's the sound of safety. That's the sound of survival. That's the sound of a seat belt locking in place. Seat belts save lives and that's a fact. That's why I don't drive anywhere until mine is on tight. Choosing to wear your seat belt is a simple as choosing between life and death. Which one do you choose?

Think about it. When you're driving in a car, you may be going 60 MPH or faster. That car is zipping down the road. Then somebody ahead of you locks up his or her brakes. Your driver doesn't have time to stop. The car that you are in crashes. Your car was going 60 miles per hour. Now, it has suddenly stopped. Your body, however, is still going 60 MPH. What's going to stop your body? Will it be the windshield or your seat belt? Every time that you get into a car you make that choice. I choose the seat belt.

Some people think that seat belts are uncool. They think that seat belts cramp their style, or that seat belts are uncomfortable. To them I say, what's more uncomfortable? Wearing a seat belt or flying through a car windshield? What's more uncool? Being safely anchored to a car, or skidding across the road in your jean shorts? Wearing a seat belt is both cooler and more comfortable than the alternatives.

Let's just take a closer look at your choices. If you are not wearing your seat belt, you can hop around the car and slide in and out of your seat easily. That sounds like a lot of fun. But, you are also more likely to die or suffer serious injuries. If you are wearing a seat belt, you have to stay in your seat. That's no fun. But, you are much more likely to walk away unharmed from a car accident. Hmmm... A small pleasure for a serious pain. That's a tough choice. I think that I'll avoid the serious pain.

How about giving money away? Do you like to give your money away? Probably not. And when you don't wear your seat belt, you are begging to give your money away. That's because kids are required to wear seat belts in every state in America. If you're riding in a car, and you don't have a seat belt on, the police can give you or your driver a ticket. Then you will have to give money to the city. I'd rather keep my money, but you can spend yours how you want.

Wearing a seat belt does not make you invincible. You can still get hurt or killed while wearing your seat belt. But wearing them has proven to be safer than driving without them. You are much less likely to be killed in a car wreck if you are wearing a seat belt. You are much less likely to get seriously injured if you are wearing one. So why not take the safer way? Why not go the way that has been proven to result in fewer deaths? You do want to live, don't you?

13. Which title best expresses the main idea of this text?
    (A) Car Accidents: Ways That We Can Prevent Them
    (B) Slow Down: Save Lives By Driving Slower
    (C) Seat Belts: Wear Them to Survive Any Wreck
    (D) Why Not? Improve Your Odds with Seat Belts

14. Which best expresses the author's main purpose in writing this text?
    (A) To inform readers about seat belt laws
    (B) To persuade readers to wear seat belts
    (C) To entertain readers with stories and jokes about seat belts
    (D) To describe what car accidents are like without seat belts

15. Which best defines the word alternatives as it is used in the third paragraph?
    (A) Being safe   (B) Being unsafe
    (C) Other choices   (D) Driving fast

16. Which statement would the author most likely agree with?
    (A) Being safe is more important than being cool.
    (B) Moving freely around a car is worth the risks.
    (C) Seat belts will keep you safe in any car accident.
    (D) You should be most concerned with your comfort.

17. Which argument is not made by the author?
    (A) Not wearing a seat belt can be expensive.
    (B) Penalties for not wearing a seat belt should increase.
    (C) Seat belts keep you from flying through the windshield.
    (D) Wearing a seat belt is cooler than suffering an injury.

1.	Ⓐ Ⓑ Ⓒ Ⓓ	5.	Ⓐ Ⓑ Ⓒ Ⓓ	9.	Ⓐ Ⓑ Ⓒ Ⓓ	13	Ⓐ Ⓑ Ⓒ Ⓓ	17.	Ⓐ Ⓑ Ⓒ Ⓓ
2.	Ⓐ Ⓑ Ⓒ Ⓓ	6.	Ⓐ Ⓑ Ⓒ Ⓓ	10.	Ⓐ Ⓑ Ⓒ Ⓓ	14.	Ⓐ Ⓑ Ⓒ Ⓓ	
3.	Ⓐ Ⓑ Ⓒ Ⓓ	7.	Ⓐ Ⓑ Ⓒ Ⓓ	11.	Ⓐ Ⓑ Ⓒ Ⓓ	15.	Ⓐ Ⓑ Ⓒ Ⓓ	
4.	Ⓐ Ⓑ Ⓒ Ⓓ	8.	Ⓐ Ⓑ Ⓒ Ⓓ	12.	Ⓐ Ⓑ Ⓒ Ⓓ	16.	Ⓐ Ⓑ Ⓒ Ⓓ	

14

SPOKEN AND WRITTEN EXPRESSION; PUNCTUATIONS

LEARNING OBJECTIVES

➤ Basic concept of Punctuations
➤ Types of Punctuations

PRACTICE EXERCISE

I.   Fill in the blanks with the correct option.

1. _______ being very rich, he never shows off.
   (A) Other than   (B) Instead
   (C) Despite   (D) Otherwise

2. I am not feeling well,_____________I will come to the party.
   (A) because   (B) since
   (C) however   (D) unless

3. _____________ I had my lunch, I didn't miss the Pizza.
   (A) Although   (B) Finally
   (C) Moreover   (D) Already

4. She never helps anyone _________ having a lot of money.
   (A) otherwise   (B) inspite of
   (C) however   (D) instead

5. You shouldn't go out _________ it's raining heavily.
   (A) for   (B) because
   (C) already   (D) but

6. My mother _______ I went to the market for shopping.
   (A) or   (B) either
   (C) neither   (D) and

7. Thomas was not telling the truth. _______ he was shouting at me.
   (A) Provided   (B) Although
   (C) Moreover   (D) In order to

8. Please come on time, _________ we may miss the flight.
   (A) otherwise   (B) so
   (C) therefore   (D) but

9. We should avoid oily food ___________ be healthy.
   (A) finally
   (B) consequently
   (C) in order to
   (D) for

10. I will give you my car ____________ you come back before 5'o clock.
    (A) as   (B) although
    (C) because   (D) provided

11. ___________my mother was sleeping, I prepared tea on my own.
    (A) As   (B) Besides
    (C) Unless   (D) Despite

12. He apologised _______ his bad behavior.
    (A) for   (B) since
    (C) because   (D) as

13. He was satisfied _________ not overjoyed.
    (A) yet   (B) as
    (C) but   (D) still

14. __________ his sister, he is very naughty.
   (A) Likely   (B) Unlike
   (C) Similar   (D) Differently

15. After months of studying hard, Meeta __________ cleared IAS examination.
   (A) initially   (B) consequently
   (C) therefore   (D) finally

II. Select the correctly punctuated sentence.

16.
   (A) Spain is a beautiful country; the beache's are warm, sandy and spotlessly clean.
   (B) Spain is a beautiful country: the beaches are warm, sandy and spotlessly clean.
   (C) Spain is a beautiful country, the beaches are warm, sandy and spotlessly clean.
   (D) Spain is a beautiful country; the beaches are warm, sandy and spotlessly clean.

17.
   (A) The children's books were all left in the following places: Mrs. Smith's room, Mr. Powell's office and the caretaker's cupboard.
   (B) The children's books were all left in the following places; Mrs. Smith's room, Mr. Powell's office and the caretaker's cupboard.
   (C) The childrens books were all left in the following places: Mrs. Smiths room, Mr. Powells office and the caretakers cupboard.
   (D) The children's books were all left in the following places, Mrs. Smith's room, Mr. Powell's office and the caretaker's cupboard.

18.
   (A) She always enjoyed sweets, chocolate, marshmallows and toffee apples.
   (B) She always enjoyed: sweets, chocolate, marshmallows and toffee apples.
   (C) She always enjoyed sweets chocolate marshmallows and toffee apples.
   (D) She always enjoyed sweet's, chocolate, marshmallow's and toffee apple's.

19.
   (A) Sarah's uncle's car was found without its wheels in that old derelict warehouse.
   (B) Sarah's uncle's car was found without its wheels in that old, derelict warehouse.
   (C) Sarahs uncles car was found without its wheels in that old, derelict warehouse.
   (D) Sarah's uncle's car was found without it's wheels in that old, derelict warehouse.

20.
   (A) I can't see Tim's car, there must have been an accident.
   (B) I cant see Tim's car; there must have been an accident.
   (C) I can't see Tim's car there must have been an accident.
   (D) I can't see Tim's car; there must have been an accident.

21.
   (A) Paul's neighbours were terrible; so his brother's friends went round to have a word.
   (B) Paul's neighbours were terrible: so his brother's friends went round to have a word.
   (C) Paul's neighbours were terrible, so his brother's friends went round to have a word.
   (D) Paul's neighbours were terrible so his brother's friends went round to have a word.

22.
   (A) Tims gran, a formidable woman, always bought him chocolate, cakes, sweets and a nice fresh apple.

(B) Tim's gran a formidable woman always bought him chocolate, cakes, sweets and a nice fresh apple.

(C) Tim's gran, a formidable woman, always bought him chocolate cakes sweets and a nice fresh apple.

(D) Tim's gran, a formidable woman, always bought him chocolate, cakes, sweets and a nice fresh apple.

23.

(A) After stealing Tims car, the thief lost his way and ended up the chief constable's garage.

(B) After stealing Tim's car the thief lost his way and ended up the chief constable's garage.

(C) After stealing Tim's car, the thief lost his way and ended up the chief constable's garage.

(D) After stealing Tim's car, the thief lost his' way and ended up the chief constable's garage.

24.

(A) We decided to visit: Spain, Greece, Portugal and Italy's mountains.

(B) We decided to visit Spain, Greece, Portugal and Italys mountains.

(C) We decided to visit Spain, Greece, Portugal and Italy's mountains.

(D) We decided to visit Spain Greece Portugal and Italy's mountains.

25.

(A) That tall man, Paul's grandad, is this month's winner.

(B) That tall man Paul's grandad is this month's winner.

(C) That tall man, Paul's grandad, is this months winner.

(D) That tall man, Pauls grandad, is this month's winner.

III. Choose the correct option for the following questions.

26. Which of the following comma rules is incorrect?

(A) Place commas after introductory elements in sentences.

(B) Place commas after items in a series.

(C) Place a comma before coordinating conjunctions that join independent clauses.

(D) Set off restrictive, essential elements with commas.

27. Which of the following possessives is correctly punctuated?

(A) The library lost all its books.

(B) That's anyones' guess.

(C) That car is not your's.

(D) That car is not their's

28. Which types of punctuation are generally used to separate independent clauses in declarative sentences in academic writing?

(A) commas and quotation marks

(B) periods and semi-colons

(C) commas and periods

(D) colons and quotation marks

29. How many commas should the following sentence contain?

"He stops fights ejects drunks soothes hysteria cures headaches and tends bar." John Steinbeck, Cannery Row

(A) one   (B) two

(C) three   (D) four

30. Which of the following sentences contains a comma error?

(A) While Washington managed to lose most of the battles he engaged in, he also managed to win the war.

(B) The loss of New York City and Philadelphia in 1777 should have ended the rebellion, but four years later, George Washington stood upon a battlefield in Virginia watching Britain's most powerful army in the colonies parade past him in surrender.

(C) We have put Washington's image on monuments and mountains, on currency and coins, and on stamps and postmarks; we have filled our country, our pockets, and our envelopes with memorials large and small to this essential man.

(D) Washington's greatest quality might have been his belief in his own abilities, in the lesser men who served with him, that attribute all too often led to personal failure and military disaster.

HOTS (ACHIEVERS SECTION)

I. Choose the correct option based on the instructions provided.

31. Choose the correct closing:
    (A) Sincerely yours:
    (B) Sincerely Yours,
    (C) Sincerely yours,
    (D) Sincerely Yours:

32. Choose the correct sentence:
    (A) Employees of the Company were laid off with little hope of returning to work.
    (B) Employees of the company were laid off with little hope of returning to work.
    (C) Employees of the company were Laid Off with little hope of returning to work.

33. Choose the correct sentence:
    (A) "You must understand," he pleaded, "That I need more time to pay you."
    (B) "You must understand," he pleaded, "that I need more time to pay you."
    (C) "You must understand," he pleaded. "That I need more time to pay you."

34. Choose the correct sentence:
    (A) Mark Paxton, the Vice President of the Company, embezzled over one million dollars.
    (B) Mark Paxton, the Vice President of the company, embezzled over one million dollars.
    (C) Mark paxton, the vice president of the company, embezzled over one million dollars.
    (D) Mark Paxton, the vice president of the company, embezzled over one million dollars.

35. Choose the correct sentence:
    (A) The West, especially California, is famous for its cutting-edge technology.
    (B) The west, especially California, is famous for its cutting-edge technology.

———Darken Your Choice with HB Pencil———

1. Ⓐ Ⓑ Ⓒ Ⓓ	8. Ⓐ Ⓑ Ⓒ Ⓓ	15. Ⓐ Ⓑ Ⓒ Ⓓ	22. Ⓐ Ⓑ Ⓒ Ⓓ	29. Ⓐ Ⓑ Ⓒ Ⓓ
2. Ⓐ Ⓑ Ⓒ Ⓓ	9. Ⓐ Ⓑ Ⓒ Ⓓ	16. Ⓐ Ⓑ Ⓒ Ⓓ	23. Ⓐ Ⓑ Ⓒ Ⓓ	30. Ⓐ Ⓑ Ⓒ Ⓓ
3. Ⓐ Ⓑ Ⓒ Ⓓ	10. Ⓐ Ⓑ Ⓒ Ⓓ	17. Ⓐ Ⓑ Ⓒ Ⓓ	24. Ⓐ Ⓑ Ⓒ Ⓓ	31. Ⓐ Ⓑ Ⓒ Ⓓ
4. Ⓐ Ⓑ Ⓒ Ⓓ	11. Ⓐ Ⓑ Ⓒ Ⓓ	18. Ⓐ Ⓑ Ⓒ Ⓓ	25. Ⓐ Ⓑ Ⓒ Ⓓ	32. Ⓐ Ⓑ Ⓒ Ⓓ
5. Ⓐ Ⓑ Ⓒ Ⓓ	12. Ⓐ Ⓑ Ⓒ Ⓓ	19. Ⓐ Ⓑ Ⓒ Ⓓ	26. Ⓐ Ⓑ Ⓒ Ⓓ	33. Ⓐ Ⓑ Ⓒ Ⓓ
6. Ⓐ Ⓑ Ⓒ Ⓓ	13. Ⓐ Ⓑ Ⓒ Ⓓ	20. Ⓐ Ⓑ Ⓒ Ⓓ	27. Ⓐ Ⓑ Ⓒ Ⓓ	34. Ⓐ Ⓑ Ⓒ Ⓓ
7. Ⓐ Ⓑ Ⓒ Ⓓ	14. Ⓐ Ⓑ Ⓒ Ⓓ	21. Ⓐ Ⓑ Ⓒ Ⓓ	28. Ⓐ Ⓑ Ⓒ Ⓓ	35. Ⓐ Ⓑ Ⓒ Ⓓ

MODEL TEST PAPER

1. Identify the misspelt word.
   (A) Remand   (B) Command
   (C) Reccomend   (D) Commend

For questions 2 and 3, choose the word with same or similar meaning to the underlined word.

2. The <u>zealous</u> politician made promises that he knew he could not possibly keep.
   (A) Jealous   (B) Enthusiastic
   (C) Fantastic   (D) Callous

3. She is suffering from a <u>chronic</u> chest infection.
   (A) Fatal   (B) Genetic
   (C) Prolonged   (D) Untreatable

For questions 4 and 5, choose the word with opposite meaning to the underlined word.

4. Socrates was <u>profound</u> and eloquent and spoke straight from the depths of his heart.
   (A) Unimpressive   (B) Superficial
   (C) Artificial   (D) Controversial

5. The women were singing in <u>melancholy</u> tones.
   (A) Amused   (B) Dismal
   (C) Cheerful   (D) Hoarse

For questions 6 to 14, choose the best option.

6. Somebody who is respected because of age or some distinction, called.
   (A) eminent
   (B) illustrious
   (C) prominent
   (D) venerable

7. Mr. Watson, my new neighbour, is such a pain in the —
   (A) neck   (B) mind
   (C) heart   (D) head

8. Someone who watches too much TV, sitting or lying down, is called:
   (A) a mouse potato   (B) a hot potato
   (C) a small potato   (D) a couch potato

9. The fiftieth anniversary of any event is called .
   (A) Silver Jubilee
   (B) Golden Jubilee
   (C) Diamond Jubilee
   (D) Platinum Jubilee

10. After his father's death, Tim had to look — the family business.
    (A) after   (B) into
    (C) at   (D) up

11. Mr. Wilson is — old to take the stairs to his fifth floor apartment.
    (A) much   (B) very
    (C) so   (D) too

12. The musician was playing the final piece when we — the auditorium.
    (A) were to enter
    (B) had entered
    (C) have entered
    (D) entered

13. 'Maria, can you find out the baby is crying? Does she need a change?'
    (A) where   (B) when
    (C) why   (D) how

14. It's definitely something to aspire .
    (A) of   (B) to
    (C) by   (D) with

For questions 15 to 19, choose the part of the sentence that has an error.

15.
   (A) Yesterday,
   (B) Bryan bought a new car
   (C) and drives it
   (D) to his home in Hong Kong.

16.
   (A) I'll visit you
   (B) when I will come
   (C) to Chennai
   (D) next week.

17.
   (A) She has
   (B) a
   (C) good news
   (D) for you.

18.
   (A) Vibhor
   (B) is married
   (C) with
   (D) a dentist.

19.
   (A) I have been
   (B) waiting for you
   (C) since
   (D) more than two hours.

For questions 20 to 24, read the passage and answer the questions that follow.

Volunteers Set the Mood of the Games

Olympic Gold Medallist Rower Katherine Grainger was born and bred in Glasgow and strongly believes that people have got a great sense of humour. Speaking of the importance of volunteers in the forthcoming Commonwealth Games, she says, "I think that a sense of humour is really a huge requirement for a lot of the volunteer roles, especially in sports festivals. I reckon, it is more important than any previous experience of volunteering." She is very confident that the organisers will get plenty of right people for volunteering that everyone will get a chance to savour Scottish humour.

The volunteers she remembers most from London Olympics 2012 were those individuals with their own personalities. "You could never say that the Games Makers were a production line of certain people. They were different ages and from different backgrounds, and they'd all welcome you in a different way," she says.

An interesting incident, she recalls her encounter with a volunteer boy in the London Olympics 2012. When she turned up on the morning of her rowing final, a volunteer welcomed her and other team members and pointing to the chocolate medal in his neck, jokingly commented, 'Hey everyone, I bet you're jealous of my gold medal!' She and her team members could not help smiling.

Another thing about the London Olympics 2012 that left her particularly impressed were the long chains of volunteers on the way to and from the stadiums. The way they were high-fiving people, dancing and singing was the most amazing sight. They enhanced the excitement and gaiety of the extravaganza and painted a very positive picture of their country, she recalls. Commenting on the general notion that volunteering may be a thankless job, she says, "Some of the volunteering roles could perhaps have been seen as mundane or not particularly glamorous, but I believe volunteering is a crucial job and that volunteers should be made to feel admired, respected and loved. That would make them even happier to be doing those roles and rub off the feel-good spirit on everyone else."

"Volunteers can really set the mood of the Games. If you get it right, people arrive and leave happy," she says.

20. What kind of people, according to Katherine, are just right for volunteering?
   (A) People who were born in Glasgow.
   (B) People who can make others laugh.
   (C) People who have experience of volunteering.
   (D) People who understand Scottish humour.

21. A quality of the volunteers of London Olympics 2012 does Katherine remember most is the.
   (A) similarities in their personalities and behaviour
   (B) uniformity in their ages and backgrounds
   (C) distinct character and conduct of each member
   (D) common way in which they welcomed guests

22. The volunteer boy with a chocolate medal in his neck was trying to—Katherine and her teammates.
   (A) Please   (B) taunt
   (C) incite   (D) flatter

23. According to paragraph 4, Katherine was most impressed with the:
   (A) extraordinary atmosphere of celebration that prevailed in the games
   (B) way volunteers added to the charm and enthusiasm of the games
   (C) amount of respect and affection that volunteers get from one and all
   (D) extraordinarily large crowds of spectators that thronged the stadiums

24. The general view about most jobs of volunteering is that they are very .
   (A) stylish and very beautiful
   (B) ordinary and unrewarding
   (C) crucial jobs few can do well
   (D) interesting and happy jobs

For questions 25 to 29, read the passage and answer the questions thatfollow.

16-Feet Waves-Where There Was Once Only Ice!

i.   National Geographic correspondent Jane J. Lee in a recent article describes how reduced sea ice has allowed the build-up of huge waves in the Beaufort Sea. She talks of sea waves as high as 16-feet in the Arctic Ocean where there was once only ice. Her fear is that because wave action breaks up sea ice, allowing more sunlight to warm the ocean, can trigger a cycle that leads to even less ice, more wind, and higher waves.

ii. According to Jane, scientists had hitherto never measured waves in the Beaufort Sea, an area north of Alaska because of the perpetual sheet of ice that prevented their formation. But, much of the region, she says, is now ice-free by September, and researchers have, as a result, been able to anchor a sensor to measure wave heights in the central Beaufort Sea in 2012.

iii. An alarming point that Jane raises is that if winds are free to blow for a longer distance over the open ocean, they can produce higher and higher waves. Sea ice restricts how far winds can blow, thus limits the formation of waves. The loss of this cover is, therefore, a cause of great concern.

iv. Jane talks of how scientists predict that in future larger waves may be rising, if the seasonal ice cover in the Arctic, continues to diminish.

v.   If that happens, it will have serious implications for the world—shorelines may be getting hit with larger and larger waves, and could erode rapidly. Moreover, reduced ice cover could also alter the amount of carbon dioxide being exchanged between the atmosphere and the ocean. As a result, the Arctic may be releasing more greenhouse gas into the atmosphere.

vi. The amount of open water, Jane says, varies annually in the Beaufort. There is virtually no open water in April, when sea ice is at its maximum, but during sea ice minimums in September, it spreads over an area of 621 miles (1,000 kilometres). Although, the Arctic has been steadily losing its sea ice cover since the late 1970s that loss was particularly quick in 2002. The 16-feet waves the scientists' instrument picked up occurred during a powerful storm on September 18, 2012.

25. What gave rise to waves in the Beaufort Sea?
   (A) Scientific studies going on there.
   (B) Presence of gentle winds in the area.
   (C) Less sea ice due to warmer climate.
   (D) A shorter summer season.

26. Until recently scientists had not measured the sea waves in the Beaufort Sea because of .
   (A) its ice-free summers
   (B) its permanent ice-cover
   (C) their failure to deploy sensors there
   (D) the particularly bad weather there

27. In third paragraph of the passage suggests that the formation of waves can be limited if somehow.
   (A) the ice cover on the sea is further reduced

(B) scientists carry out more studies in the area

(C) winds can travel longer distance over the open sea

(D) winds are not allowed to travel long distances

28. Larger waves in the Arctic, in future, may result in .
(A) reduced CO2 exchange between the ocean and the atmosphere
(B) no open water in the Arctic in summer season
(C) wider, thicker ice cover in winters in the Arctic
(D) discharge of more greenhouse gases in the atmosphere

29. The year saw an increase in the speed at which the loss of the Arctic ice-cover occurred.
(A) 1970   (B) 1972
(C) 2002   (D) 2012

For questions 30 to 34, choose the best option.

30. You say 'You've got to be kidding me' when you doubt that someone is .
(A) pretending to be a kid
(B) worrying too much
(C) not speaking the truth
(D) trying to be extra polite

31. If you want someone else to go ahead of you or pass through ahead of you, which of the following expressions would you use?
(A) You first, please.
(B) After you, please.
(C) First you, please.
(D) Go before me, please.

32. If someone says, 'No worries', he/she wants to say ' '.
(A) I'm a carefree person
(B) there is nothing to lose
(C) that's all right
(D) what will happen, will happen

33. If you don't hear something properly, you can politely request the speaker to repeat what they said, by using the expression?
(A) What?
(B) Repeat.
(C) Come again, please.
(D) Once again.

34. After hours of struggle, when Bob finally succeeded in starting the car, Mary shouted in great excitement, ' !'
(A) What the hell
(B) Way to go
(C) Oh, no
(D) What the Dickens

For questions 35 to 43, choose the best option to fill in the blanks.

Delhi's Latest Tourist Attraction: Delhi Eye

Years after its construction, New Delhi's (35) tourist attraction, Delhi Eye is (36) open to public. Constructed (37) the famous flyers in London and Singapore, it has been created by the same Dutch company that made the Singapore Flyer. (38) an 18-storey building (45 metres or 200 feet), this Ferris wheel has cost approximately £7 million and has a total capacity of 288 people. Its 36 air-conditioned cabins offer a (39) view of the popular sites in the vicinity – (40) Akshardham Temple, Humayun's Tom and Lotus Temple, all in (41) of 20 minutes.

On a (42) day, one can even see Connaught Place from a distance. Its observatory-style experience would be special for the visitors, since the (43) view over Delhi is spectacular.

35.
(A) lost   (B) last
(C) later   (D) latest

36.
(A) newly   (B) partially
(C) initially   (D) finally

37.
(A) along the lines of
(B) in line with
(C) out of line with
(D) on the right lines

38.
    (A) So tall as
    (B) As tall as
    (C) More tall than
    (D) Much taller than

39.
    (A) naked eye   (B) worm's eye
    (C) bird's eye   (D) satellite's

40.
    (A) include   (B) includes
    (C) included   (D) including

41.
    (A) an interval   (B) an area
    (C) a span   (D) a section

42.
    (A) hazy   (B) cloudy
    (C) clear   (D) rainy

43.
    (A) overreaching   (B) far reaching
    (C) within reach   (D) beyond reach

For questions 44 and 45, choose the correct stress pattern for the underlined words.

44. Annual _examinations_ are held in the month of June every year.
    (A) EXaminations   (B) exaMInations
    (C) examiNAtions   (D) examinaTIons

45. That's an interesting _activity_.
    (A) ACTivity   (B) acTIvity
    (C) actiVIty   (D) activiTY

46. Identify the misspelt word.
    (A) Dyeing   (B) Fungi
    (C) Sking   (D) Taxing

47. Choose the part of the sentence that has an error.
    (A) She wants
    (B) to know
    (C) why
    (D) is the baby crying.

48. Choose the correct stress pattern for the underlined word.

She is a well-known _choreographer_ of the film industry.
    (A) CHOreographer
    (B) choreOgrapher
    (C) choreoGRAPHer
    (D) choreographER

For questions 49 and 50, choose the best option.

49. Someone who can speak many languages is called a/an .
    (A) orator   (B) linguistics
    (C) polyglot   (D) ventriloquist

50. If at a restaurant your friends say, 'Let's go Dutch', they mean to say that .
    (A) only one of the members will pay for all
    (B) they wish to try some Dutch dishes
    (C) they wish to eat in the way, the Dutch eat
    (D) everyone will pay for himself or herself

—Darken Your Choice with HB Pencil—

1. Ⓐ Ⓑ Ⓒ Ⓓ	11. Ⓐ Ⓑ Ⓒ Ⓓ	21. Ⓐ Ⓑ Ⓒ Ⓓ	31. Ⓐ Ⓑ Ⓒ Ⓓ	41. Ⓐ Ⓑ Ⓒ Ⓓ
2. Ⓐ Ⓑ Ⓒ Ⓓ	12. Ⓐ Ⓑ Ⓒ Ⓓ	22. Ⓐ Ⓑ Ⓒ Ⓓ	32. Ⓐ Ⓑ Ⓒ Ⓓ	42. Ⓐ Ⓑ Ⓒ Ⓓ
3. Ⓐ Ⓑ Ⓒ Ⓓ	13. Ⓐ Ⓑ Ⓒ Ⓓ	23. Ⓐ Ⓑ Ⓒ Ⓓ	33. Ⓐ Ⓑ Ⓒ Ⓓ	43. Ⓐ Ⓑ Ⓒ Ⓓ
4. Ⓐ Ⓑ Ⓒ Ⓓ	14. Ⓐ Ⓑ Ⓒ Ⓓ	24. Ⓐ Ⓑ Ⓒ Ⓓ	34. Ⓐ Ⓑ Ⓒ Ⓓ	44. Ⓐ Ⓑ Ⓒ Ⓓ
5. Ⓐ Ⓑ Ⓒ Ⓓ	15. Ⓐ Ⓑ Ⓒ Ⓓ	25. Ⓐ Ⓑ Ⓒ Ⓓ	35. Ⓐ Ⓑ Ⓒ Ⓓ	45. Ⓐ Ⓑ Ⓒ Ⓓ
6. Ⓐ Ⓑ Ⓒ Ⓓ	16. Ⓐ Ⓑ Ⓒ Ⓓ	26. Ⓐ Ⓑ Ⓒ Ⓓ	36. Ⓐ Ⓑ Ⓒ Ⓓ	46. Ⓐ Ⓑ Ⓒ Ⓓ
7. Ⓐ Ⓑ Ⓒ Ⓓ	17. Ⓐ Ⓑ Ⓒ Ⓓ	27. Ⓐ Ⓑ Ⓒ Ⓓ	37. Ⓐ Ⓑ Ⓒ Ⓓ	47. Ⓐ Ⓑ Ⓒ Ⓓ
8. Ⓐ Ⓑ Ⓒ Ⓓ	18. Ⓐ Ⓑ Ⓒ Ⓓ	28. Ⓐ Ⓑ Ⓒ Ⓓ	38. Ⓐ Ⓑ Ⓒ Ⓓ	48. Ⓐ Ⓑ Ⓒ Ⓓ
9. Ⓐ Ⓑ Ⓒ Ⓓ	19. Ⓐ Ⓑ Ⓒ Ⓓ	29. Ⓐ Ⓑ Ⓒ Ⓓ	39. Ⓐ Ⓑ Ⓒ Ⓓ	49. Ⓐ Ⓑ Ⓒ Ⓓ
10. Ⓐ Ⓑ Ⓒ Ⓓ	20. Ⓐ Ⓑ Ⓒ Ⓓ	30. Ⓐ Ⓑ Ⓒ Ⓓ	40. Ⓐ Ⓑ Ⓒ Ⓓ	50. Ⓐ Ⓑ Ⓒ Ⓓ

HINTS AND SOLUTIONS

1. SYNONYMS, ANTONYMS, HOMONYMS AND HOMOPHONES

Answer Key

I									
1. (D)	2. (C)	3. (B)	4. (A)	5. (A)	6. (C)	7. (D)	8. (C)	9. (C)	10. (C)

II									
11. (C)	12. (D)	13. (A)	14. (B)	15. (B)	16. (C)	17. (B)	18. (A)	19. (C)	20. (D)

III									
21. (A)	22. (B)	23. (B)	24. (B)	25. (C)	26. (B)	27. (B)	28. (A)	29. (B)	30. (A)

HOTS (ACHIEVERS SECTION)

31. (B)	32. (D)	33. (B)	34. (A)	35. (C)

2. ANALOGIES AND SPELLINGS

Answer Key

I									
1. (D)	2. (B)	3. (B)	4. (C)	5. (D)	6. (A)	7. (A)	8. (A)	9. (C)	10. (D)

II									
11. (D)	12. (C)	13. (D)	14. (C)	15. (C)	16. (B)	17. (B)	18. (C)	19. (B)	20. (C)

III									
21. (C)	22. (D)	23. (B)	24. (B)	25. (B)	26. (A)	27. (B)	28. (C)	29. (D)	30. (D)

HOTS (ACHIEVERS SECTION)

31. (C)	32. (A)	33. (D)	34. (C)	35. (B)

1. Peccadillos here means a relatively minor fault or sin.

2. Languor means tiredness or inactivity, especially when pleasurable.

3. The correct word denouement here means the final part of a play, film, or narrative in which the strands of the plot are drawn together and matters are explained or resolved.

Answer Key

I

1. (D)	2. (D)	3. (D)	4. (B)	5. (D)	6. (C)	7. (A)	8. (C)	9. (D)	10. (D)

II

11. (B)	12. (B)	13. (B)	14. (D)	15. (A)	16. (D)	17. (C)	18. (A)	19. (C)	20. (C)

III

21. (B)	22. (A)	23. (D)	24. (A)	25. (C)	26. (A)	27. (A)	28. (C)	29. (D)	30. (C)

HOTS (ACHIEVERS SECTION)

31. (B)	32. (A)	33. (D)		

4. PHRASAL VERBS, IDIOMS AND PROVERBS

Answer Key

I

1. (B)	2. (A)	3. (D)	4. (C)	5. (A)	6. (C)	7. (D)	8. (A)	9. (B)	10. (D)

II

11. (C)	12. (B)	13. (B)	14. (D)	15. (A)	16. (B)	17. (B)	18. (B)	19. (B)	20. (C)

III

21. (B)	22. (C)	23. (C)	24. (A)	25. (D)	26. (C)	27. (A)	28. (C)	29. (C)	30. (D)

HOTS (ACHIEVERS SECTION)

31. (C)	32. (C)	33. (D)	34. (C)	35. (B)

5. NOUNS AND PRONOUNS

Answer Key

I

1. (C)	2. (B)	3. (A)	4. (C)	5. (B)	6. (B)	7. (A)	8. (A)	9. (C)	10. (A)

II

11. (B)	12. (B)	13. (A)	14. (A)	15. (B)					

III

16. (B)	17. (B)	18. (A)	19. (C)	20. (A)					

				IV					
21. (A)	22. (A)	23. (A)	24. (B)	25. (A)	26. (A)	27. (A)	28. (A)	29. (A)	30. (A)

HOTS (ACHIEVERS SECTION)

31. (B)	32. (B)	33. (B)	34. (C)	35. (A)

6. VERBS AND ADVERBS

Answer Key

				I					
1. (D)	2. (A)	3. (B)	4. (D)	5. (B)	6. (C)	7. (C)	8. (A)	9. (D)	10. (A)

				II					
11. (B)	12. (C)	13. (D)	14. (A)	15. (B)					

				III					
16. (A)	17. (C)	18. (B)	19. (A)	20. (C)					

				IV					
21. (A)	22. (C)	23. (A)	24. (C)	25. (C)					

				V					
26. (A)	27. (D)	28. (D)	29. (A)	30. (C)					

HOTS (ACHIEVERS SECTION)

31. (B)	32. (C)	33. (A)	34. (D)	35. (A)

7. ADJECTIVES

Answer Key

				I					
1. (B)	2. (A)	3. (A)	4. (C)	5. (C)	6. (C)	7. (A)	8. (A)	9. (C)	10. (C)

				II					
11. (B)	12. (C)	13. (A)	14. (C)	15. (A)	16. (A)	17. (B)	18. (B)	19. (A)	20. (B)

HOTS (ACHIEVERS SECTION)

21. (C)	22. (A)	23. (D)	24. (C)	25. (C)

8. ARTICLES AND PREPOSITIONS

Answer Key

I									
1. (A)	2. (C)	3. (B)	4. (A)	5. (C)	6. (B)	7. (A)	8. (A)	9. (A)	10. (C)

II									
11. (A)	12. (D)	13. (B)	14. (B)	15. (C)	16. (A)	17. (A)	18. (A)	19. (C)	20. (D)

III									
21. (B)	22. (B)	23. (A)	24. (C)	25. (D)					

IV									
26. (B)	27. (C)	28. (B)	29. (B)	30. (A)					

HOTS (ACHIEVERS SECTION)

31. (D)	32. (C)	33. (B)	34. (A)	35. (C)

9. CONJUNCTIONS AND DETERMINERS

Answer Key

1. (B)	2. (B)	3. (A)	4. (C)	5. (C)	6. (B)	7. (B)	8. (C)	9. (A)	10. (B)
11. (D)	12. (C)	13. (B)	14. (C)	15. (B)	16. (C)	17. (A)	18. (A)	19. (B)	20. (B)

HOTS (ACHIEVERS SECTION)

21. (C)	22. (A)	23. (D)	24. (C)	25. (B)

10. JUMBLED WORDS

Answer Key

1. (C)	2. (B)	3. (C)	4. (A)	5. (C)	6. (B)	7. (B)	8. (A)	9. (A)	10. (C)
11. (A)	12. (C)	13. (B)	14. (A)	15. (C)	16. (B)	17. (B)	18. (A)	19. (C)	20. (C)

HOTS (ACHIEVERS SECTION)

21. (D)	22. (C)	23. (B)	24. (D)	25. (A)

Answer Key

I

1. (C)	2. (A)	3. (C)	4. (C)	5. (A)	6. (A)	7. (B)	8. (A)	9. (B)	10. (B)

II

11. (A)	12. (B)	13. (B)	14. (C)	15. (D)	16. (A)	17. (B)	18. (C)	19. (A)	20. (D)

III

21. (A)	22. (C)	23. (B)	24. (C)	25. (C)	26. (B)	27. (A)	28. (D)	29. (B)	30. (B)

HOTS (ACHIEVERS SECTION)

31. HAVE HAD	32. HAVE LOVED	33. HAVE BEEN THINKING, HAVE BECOME	34. HAS BEEN WORKING, HAS ENJOYED	35. HAVE YOU BEEN

12. VOICE AND NARRATION

Answer Key

I

1. (B)	2. (B)	3. (B)	4. (B)	5. (A)	6. (B)	7. (C)	8. (B)	9. (A)	10. (A)

II

11. (B)	12. (B)	13. (C)	14. (B)	15. (B)					

III

16. (B)	17. (C)	18. (B)	19. (A)	20. (C)					

IV

21. (A)	22. (A)	23. (C)	24. (A)	25. (C)					

V

26. (C)	27. (B)	28. (B)	29. (A)	30. (B)					

HOTS (ACHIEVERS SECTION)

31. (A)	32. (D)	33. (A)	34. (D)	35. (A)

Answer Key

I

1. (B)	2. (A)	3. (D)	4. (C)	5. (A)	6. (E)	7. (B)			

II

8. THE PROJECT CALLED 'ROAD TO FREEDOM FROM POLLUTION' HAS BEEN LAUNCHED BY PM MODI

9. THE EXPRESSWAY WILL DO AWAY WITH 31 TRAFFIC SIGNALS.

10. THE NEW ROAD WILL SAVE 1 HOUR 50 MINUTES AFTER IT IS READY TO USE.

11. MR. ATAL BIHARI BAJPAYEE JI LAUNCHED TWO PROJECTS.

12. THE TOTAL COST OF THE PROJECT IS RS. 7500 CRORES.

HOTS (ACHIEVERS SECTION)

13. (D)	14. (B)	15. (C)	16. (A)	17. (B)

14. SPOKEN AND WRITTEN EXPRESSION; PUNCTUATIONS

Answer Key

I

1. (C)	2. (C)	3. (A)	4. (B)	5. (B)	6. (D)	7. (C)	8. (A)	9. (C)	10. (D)
11. (A)	12. (A)	13. (C)	14. (B)	15. (D)					

II

16. (D)	17. (A)	18. (A)	19. (B)	20. (D)	21. (C)	22. (C)	23. (B)	24. (C)	25. (A)

III

26. (D)	27. (A)	28. (B)	29. (D)	30. (D)					

HOTS (ACHIEVERS SECTION)

31. (B)	32. (B)	33. (B)	34. (D)	35. (A)

Answer Key

1. (C)	2. (B)	3. (D)	4. (D)	5. (B)	6. (C)	7. (D)	8. (D)	9. (D)	10. (B)
11. (A)	12. (B)	13. (B)	14. (A)	15. (D)	16. (C)	17. (B)	18. (A)	19. (C)	20. (C)
21. (C)	22. (D)	23. (B)	24. (C)	25. (B)	26. (B)	27. (C)	28. (C)	29. (D)	30. (B)
31. (A)	32. (B)	33. (D)	34. (B)	35. (D)	36. (B)	37. (D)	38. (C)	39. (B)	40. (C)
41. (A)	42. (C)	43. (C)	44. (A)	45. (C)	46. (B)	47. (B)	48. (B)	49. (C)	50. (C)

SAMPLE OMR ANSWER SHEET

1. STUDENT NAME (IN ENGLISH CAPITAL LETTERS ONLY)

Students must write and darken the respective circles completely using HB Pencil only. Othewise their Answer Sheets will not be evaluated.

PERSONAL DETAILS

2. SCHOOL CODE

3. CLASS

4. SECTION

5. ROLL NO.

6. QUESTION PAPER SET

A ○
B ○
C ○
D ○

7. MOBILE NUMBER

8. GENDER

MALE ○
FEMALE ○

9. STREAM
(Only for Class XI and XII Students)

MATHEMATICS ○
BIOLOGY ○
OTHERS ○

MARK YOUR ANSWERS

1.	Ⓐ Ⓑ Ⓒ Ⓓ	26.	Ⓐ Ⓑ Ⓒ Ⓓ
2.	Ⓐ Ⓑ Ⓒ Ⓓ	27.	Ⓐ Ⓑ Ⓒ Ⓓ
3.	Ⓐ Ⓑ Ⓒ Ⓓ	28.	Ⓐ Ⓑ Ⓒ Ⓓ
4.	Ⓐ Ⓑ Ⓒ Ⓓ	29.	Ⓐ Ⓑ Ⓒ Ⓓ
5.	Ⓐ Ⓑ Ⓒ Ⓓ	30.	Ⓐ Ⓑ Ⓒ Ⓓ
6.	Ⓐ Ⓑ Ⓒ Ⓓ	31.	Ⓐ Ⓑ Ⓒ Ⓓ
7.	Ⓐ Ⓑ Ⓒ Ⓓ	32.	Ⓐ Ⓑ Ⓒ Ⓓ
8.	Ⓐ Ⓑ Ⓒ Ⓓ	33.	Ⓐ Ⓑ Ⓒ Ⓓ
9.	Ⓐ Ⓑ Ⓒ Ⓓ	34.	Ⓐ Ⓑ Ⓒ Ⓓ
10.	Ⓐ Ⓑ Ⓒ Ⓓ	35.	Ⓐ Ⓑ Ⓒ Ⓓ
11.	Ⓐ Ⓑ Ⓒ Ⓓ	36.	Ⓐ Ⓑ Ⓒ Ⓓ
12.	Ⓐ Ⓑ Ⓒ Ⓓ	37.	Ⓐ Ⓑ Ⓒ Ⓓ
13.	Ⓐ Ⓑ Ⓒ Ⓓ	38.	Ⓐ Ⓑ Ⓒ Ⓓ
14.	Ⓐ Ⓑ Ⓒ Ⓓ	39.	Ⓐ Ⓑ Ⓒ Ⓓ
15.	Ⓐ Ⓑ Ⓒ Ⓓ	40.	Ⓐ Ⓑ Ⓒ Ⓓ
16.	Ⓐ Ⓑ Ⓒ Ⓓ	41.	Ⓐ Ⓑ Ⓒ Ⓓ
17.	Ⓐ Ⓑ Ⓒ Ⓓ	42.	Ⓐ Ⓑ Ⓒ Ⓓ
18.	Ⓐ Ⓑ Ⓒ Ⓓ	43.	Ⓐ Ⓑ Ⓒ Ⓓ
19.	Ⓐ Ⓑ Ⓒ Ⓓ	44.	Ⓐ Ⓑ Ⓒ Ⓓ
20.	Ⓐ Ⓑ Ⓒ Ⓓ	45.	Ⓐ Ⓑ Ⓒ Ⓓ
21.	Ⓐ Ⓑ Ⓒ Ⓓ	46.	Ⓐ Ⓑ Ⓒ Ⓓ
22.	Ⓐ Ⓑ Ⓒ Ⓓ	47.	Ⓐ Ⓑ Ⓒ Ⓓ
23.	Ⓐ Ⓑ Ⓒ Ⓓ	48.	Ⓐ Ⓑ Ⓒ Ⓓ
24.	Ⓐ Ⓑ Ⓒ Ⓓ	49.	Ⓐ Ⓑ Ⓒ Ⓓ
25.	Ⓐ Ⓑ Ⓒ Ⓓ	50.	Ⓐ Ⓑ Ⓒ Ⓓ

Signature of the Student & Date of Examination

Signature of the Invigilator & Date of Examination

V&S Publishers, F-2/16 Ansari Road, Daryaganj, New Delhi-110002, ☎ 011-23240026-27
✉ info@vspublishers.com, 🌐 www.vspublishers.com